On Editing Old French Texts

The scribe ends Chrétien de Troyes's *Yvain* in the left column and begins his *Lancelot* with a large *D* at the top of the right column. In the miniature, Méléagant defies King Arthur.

Princeton University Library, Garrett MS 125, fol. 34r.

On Editing
Old French Texts

Alfred Foulet
and
Mary Blakely Speer

THE REGENTS PRESS OF KANSAS
Lawrence

Library of Congress Cataloging in Publication Data

Foulet, Alfred Lucien, 1900–
On editing Old French texts.

Bibliography: p.
Includes index.
1. French literature—To 1500—Criticism, Textual.
2. Manuscripts, French—Editing.
3. French language—To 1500.
4. Paleography, French.
I. Speer, Mary Blakely, 1942–   joint author.
II. Title.
PA155.T48F6   808'.02'0944   78-13151
ISBN 0-7006-0182-1

This volume initiates a new scholarly series, The Edward C. Armstrong Monographs on Medieval Literature, under the general editorship of Karl D. Uitti of Princeton University.

Contents

vi

Foreword

It is entirely fitting that this volume should initiate a new scholarly series: The Edward C. Armstrong Monographs on Medieval Literature. The late Professor Armstrong, who for so many years edited the Elliott Monographs in the Romance Languages and Literatures with great distinction, was Alfred Foulet's teacher at Princeton, where, more recently, Foulet directed the graduate work of Professor Speer.

Yet this series is not meant merely to be a continuation of the older venture under a new name. Its scope and purposes differ from those of the Elliott Monographs, though, of course, we intend to derive inspiration from, and to respect, the high standards and scholarly integrity displayed by the earlier enterprise. Our outlook, both in methodology and in coverage, will be somewhat broader than that of our Romance-based predecessor. Thus, for this series, "medieval literature" signifies the medieval literatures of Latin, Romance, and Germanic Europe as well as of Eastern Christendom, Islam, and the Jewish traditions; and the series will focus on the millennium spanning the fifth through the fifteenth centuries. Even over the long run, however, we do not expect the Armstrong Monographs to provide blanket coverage of the period or of the literatures involved. We have in mind no encyclopedic global plan nor a standardized reference set. Finally, we do not seek to compete with specialized scholarly monographs or with the kind of critico-theoretical speculation so typical of medievalistic literary investigation. What we hope to provide is a series of model introductory studies that combine the needs of nonspecialists, or tyros, with the resources of specialists.

We are delighted, therefore, to open the series with the publication of *On Editing Old French Texts*. This work is a handbook, the distillation of many years of experience by countless scholars in a practice that, over the past century or so, has endowed us with the basic tools with which scholars and critics in Old French literature work today. Professors Foulet and Speer have conveniently summarized this practice—its history, its achievements, its capacities—and, in reading their book, one cannot help but marvel at the learning, the care, and the immense variety of values represented by such giants as Foerster, Bédier, and Armstrong. One understands that in editing an Old French text for modern readers the critic displays his prejudices, his tastes, even his temperament. Each edition is a commentary and, of course, must be viewed as such. There is no monolithically right way of editing. Though they do not do so explicitly, the authors nevertheless implicitly recognize what might be called the complexities of the actual establishment—or determination—of what in fact an Old French text is. Of course, for many of us these days, the determination (if there really can be one) constitutes the nexus of the problem; frequently *the* text turns out to be a number of manuscript versions, or performances, more or less interrelated and/or related to versions of other texts (as when, for example, a poem appears alongside other poems in the same codex). Generic problems and questions of textuality abound. These are matters of passionate concern and, in their way, reflect the on-going debates which, since Lachmann at least, have epitomized textual criticism.

Professors Foulet and Speer have chosen—to my mind quite rightly—to concentrate their attention on the establishment of *a/the* text in terms that take into account the needs of the modern reader while respecting the textual complexities present in specific traditions. Without the products of the kind of establishment they describe medieval literary studies could hardly exist as they now do. Serious scholarship in Old French literature must start with the kind(s) of edition Professors Foulet and Speer deal with.

Editors will find *On Editing Old French Texts* an indispensable practical guide as well as a brilliantly written history of their discipline. And, in keeping with the spirit of the Armstrong Monographs, this volume will be of particular value to beginners in the field and to such nonspecialists as would like better to understand the traditions and practices of an important branch of medievalistic philology.

Karl D. Uitti

Princeton University
May 1978

Editorial Board

Michael J. H. Curschmann
Alan D. Deyermond
John V. Fleming
Nina G. Garsoian
Andras P. Hamori
Robert B. Hollander, Jr.
Janet M. Martin
Karl D. Uitti, General Editor

Abbreviations

APF	Anciens Poëtes de la France
BBSIA	Bulletin Bibliographique de la Société Internationale Arthurienne
BEC	Bibliothèque de l'Ecole des chartes
BÉHÉ	Bibliothèque de l'Ecole des Hautes Etudes
BFR	Bibliothèque Française et Romane
Bibl. munic.	Bibliothèque municipale
B.N.	Bibliothèque Nationale
CFMA	Classiques Français du Moyen Age
EM	Elliott Monographs in the Romance Languages and Literatures
PRF	Publications Romanes et Françaises
RPh	Romance Philology
SATF	Société des Anciens Textes Français
TLF	Textes Littéraires Français
UNCSRLL	University of North Carolina Studies in Romance Languages and Literatures

Preface

For half a century now, almost all editors of Old French works—whatever the nationality of the editor—have referred to the code of practical rules for editing Old French and Old Provençal texts which Mario Roques presented to the members of the Société des Anciens Textes Français in October 1925 (published as a report, Paris, 1926; reprinted in *Romania*, 1926, 243–49, and in *BEC*, 1926, 453–59). *Practical* is the key word here, for these rules govern primarily the punctuation and layout of the printed text and the content of its accompanying apparatus; they do not touch on such troublesome matters as stemma construction or editorial philosophy. Within their limited domain, the Roques rules have provided a much-needed standard, replacing the earlier code drawn up by Paul Meyer, also for the Société des Anciens Textes Français (*Bulletin de la Société des Anciens Textes Français*, 1908, 64–79; reprinted in *BEC*, 1910, 224–33). Nevertheless, many editors have come to feel that the Roques rules are no longer adequate, and they have modified them on certain points—for example, the use of the *tréma* and the manner of representing numerals in the text.

In 1925, and for several decades to come, bitter controversy surrounded the fundamental problems ignored by the Roques rules. Basically these issues boil down to the very nature of the editor's task: whether he should try to reconstruct the author's original text or, instead, honor the redaction of the best manuscript available to him. Today Old French scholars continue to disagree on this, with the result that each editor in effect formulates his own editorial philosophy, based on the manuscript tradition of the work he wishes to edit, the arguments of other practitioners, and his own inclinations. Yet recently several scholars have tried to ease the novice editor's path by offering him both practical advice and food for theoretical thought. We have in mind particularly Franca Brambilla Ageno's dense volume, *L'edizione critica dei testi volgari* (Padua, 1975), representing the long and fruitful activist Italian tradition which stresses the editor's duty to the author; the essays collected by Christopher Kleinhenz in *Medieval Manuscripts and Textual Criticism* (Chapel Hill, 1976), which, by and large, also encourage editorial activism; and the down-to-earth procedures which Charles Moorman recommends for graduate students in *Editing the Middle English Manuscript* (Jackson, Miss., 1975). None of these books, however, deals specifically and systematically with the special problems of Old French texts.

So we think the time has come for a guidebook to aid editors and readers of Old French works. We have tried to be as comprehensive as possible, putting the thorny theoretical issues in perspective and also adapting and expanding the Roques rules to obtain more precise standards which reflect current practices and give more assistance to inexperienced editors. Part 1 of our manual provides a historical overview of Old French textual criticism from the end of the eighteenth century to the present; we analyze the editorial methods which prevailed at different times, together with representative editions from each period. In Part 2, we examine, in more or less chronological order, the tasks faced by the editor in preparing the text of his edition: collecting the materials, transcribing and collating the manuscripts, constructing a stemma, choosing a basic manuscript, grooming the text with punctuation and diacritical marks for the modern reader, and making corrections and emendations. Part 3 focuses on compiling the various sections which make up the framework accompanying a critical edition: the introduction, critical apparatus, notes, glossary, table of proper names, and so on. A list of Editors and Critical Editions cited in the manual supplies complete bibliographical data for all texts mentioned in discussions of procedures or layout; because of this, references to editions in Parts 2 and 3 usually name only the title, author, and editor. The Selective Reference Bibliography is designed as a guide for further reading in specific areas.

To keep our guidebook a manageable length, we limit our discussion and examples to texts composed in the Francien literary *koine* between about 1150 and 1300. This period is rich in literary texts, as even a cursory examination of the Bartsch-Wiese and Albert Henry anthologies shows. Excluded from our manual are archaic texts (before 1150), those composed in Middle French (after 1300), those composed in strongly marked dialects (such as Anglo-Norman), and nonliterary documents (charters, diplomas, etc.): all these require special consideration.

For whom do we write? For the novice editor of Old French texts, including the graduate student who is preparing an edition as his doctoral dissertation; for the experienced editor who seeks a convenient reference guide to supplant the Roques rules; for scholars who review critical editions in the various journals dealing with medieval French language and literature; and, more broadly, for any student or professor of Old French who uses an edition and needs to be reminded that, in all likelihood, what he is reading is not actually the author's composition but the result of hundreds of editorial decisions. We have assumed that our readers possess a good working knowledge of Old French forms and syntax and are familiar with conventions of punctuation in modern English and French.

A word about our attitudes. In practical concerns, we often tend, like the Roques rules, to be prescriptive, and we have sought to illustrate our rules and suggestions with abundant examples. In matters closer to the theoretical crux of editing, we tend to be more descriptive. We do have a point of view, which we try to make clear, but we realize that it is difficult to formulate hard rules which might apply to every text because, to a large extent, each text is a special case requiring a unique treatment. Handling such problems as variants and emendations calls for informed but necessarily subjective judgments. There we hope, on the one hand, to make the editor aware of the range and nature of his choices and, on the other, to point out to the reader what choices have been made on his behalf.

1

A Historical Orientation

I. INTRODUCTION

Preparing an edition of an Old French text is an exacting task and often a controversial one because it can seldom, if ever, be carried out mechanically. Anyone who examines several editions of the same text, especially those published thirty or forty years apart, will notice marked differences in the text itself, as well as in its accompanying apparatus. Joseph Bédier identified the two crucial forces affecting the process as the individual editor's personality and the dominant editorial philosophy of his time:

> Certaines éditions d'un ouvrage illustre s'opposent en effet à certaines autres comme le noir au blanc, et cela parce qu'elles représentent chacune, outre le tempérament individuel de celui qui la procure, un ensemble de principes plus ou moins accrédités de son temps, parfois des *idola tribus*, des modes, que les uns ont suivies, tandis que d'autres réagissent contre elles. Il est entendu que ce perpétuel renouvellement des points de vue de la critique est chose bonne et salutaire.[1]

Not everyone would agree that the occasionally bitter disputes fought in the name of theory have been salutary for the discipline, but they undeniably form part of its history. Some

---

[1] "De l'édition princeps de la *Chanson de Roland* aux éditions les plus récentes: nouvelles remarques sur l'art d'établir les anciens textes," *Romania*, 64 (1938), 152f.

1

acquaintance with the historical dimension of editing is essential for both the reader of an edited text, who needs to evaluate the editor's work accurately, and for the prospective editor, who must be able to weigh thoroughly the consequences of the myriad decisions he will have to make.

Textual criticism is the name given to that part of literary study which deals with determining the content and form of a text. Fredson Bowers defined it as "a general term for the application of logical method to analyzing the relationship between preserved and inferential forms of the text, followed by the application of various techniques, including critical judgment, designed to establish what will ordinarily be the single definitive form of the text."[2] Editing Old French texts comes under the heading of textual criticism; yet the requirements of Old French texts are sometimes exceptional, and the theories this special branch has generated have not always been countenanced by, say, editors of Cicero or of Herman Melville. Moreover, the word *definitive*, as Bowers used it, does not apply to editions of Old French texts.

In the historical survey that follows, we have tried to present, with examples, the attitudes and theories which characterized the three fairly distinct earlier periods of Old French editing (Chapters II–IV).[3] A fourth period, still under way, is not clearly separated from the third period, and its theoretical stance has not yet been defined in terms acceptable to a majority of editors; Chapter V is, then, a report on recent devel-

---

[2] "Textual Criticism," *Encyclopaedia Britannica* (Chicago, 1967), XXI, 918.

[3] To date, most historical treatments of Old French editing focus on the different editions of a single text. Of these, the most informative are by Joseph Bédier: "La tradition manuscrite du *Lai de l'Ombre*: réflexions sur l'art d'éditer les anciens textes," *Romania*, 54 (1928), 161–96, 321–56; "De l'édition princeps de la *Chanson de Roland* . . . ," *Romania*, 63 (1937), 433–69, and 64 (1938), 145–244, 489–521. The former has been reprinted as a pamphlet (Paris, 1970); the latter is complemented by Frederick Whitehead, in "The Textual Criticism of the *Chanson de Roland*: An Historical Review," *Studies . . . Alfred Ewert* (Oxford, 1961), pp. 76–89. For a wider-ranging survey, see the *état présent* by Whitehead and Cedric E. Pickford: "The Introduction to the *Lai de l'Ombre*: Sixty Years Later," *Romania*, 94 (1973), 145–56; rpt., with a slightly different title, in *Medieval Manuscripts and Textual Criticism*, ed. Christopher Kleinhenz (UNCSRLL, Symposia, 4; Chapel Hill, 1976), pp. 103–15.

opments. Detailed explanations of editorial procedures have been reserved for Part 2 of our manual.

II. THE EMPIRICAL PERIOD

Modern editions of Old French texts which were based on manuscripts rather than sixteenth-century printed editions began to appear about the middle of the eighteenth century. They were at first luxurious curiosities, appealing to historians, antiquarians, and the literarily adventurous; but as France rediscovered her pre-Renaissance past, the number of Old French editions increased, starting around 1830. In those early days there was no system for editing medieval works. The text depended on two factors: the number and quality of the manuscripts available to the editor and his skill in reading them, correcting them, and combining their various readings when they differed. The extent to which the editor modified the manuscript text varied from work to work and from editor to editor; the reader is not always told how much the editor has changed his manuscript text, or even what manuscript(s) he has followed.

As examples of early nineteenth-century editions, consider D. M. Méon's revised, expanded text of *Fabliaux et contes des poètes françois des XI, XII, XIII, XIV et XV*e *siècles, tirés des meilleurs auteurs* (4 vols.; Paris, 1808), first published by Etienne Barbazan in 1756, and Méon's *Roman de Renart* (4 vols.; Paris, 1826). In the *Fabliaux et contes* Méon declared that he had checked the 1756 edition against the manuscripts Barbazan had used in order to correct all errors of transcription; while doing so, he found new manuscripts of some *fabliaux*, and did not hesitate to add verses from them to the existing printed text. For each poem, he regularly cited the manuscripts containing it, but he neglected to indicate which ones had served as basic manuscripts; only rarely, as for *La Bible Guiot de Provins*, did he provide any variants. For the *Renart*, Méon worked with twelve manuscripts, of which he identified only six. Since the order of the branches varies in the different manuscripts, he reorganized them into a plan of his own; also, as with the *fabliaux*, he blended together the readings of all the manuscripts to give a complete and smooth text: "Autant qu'il m'a été possible, j'ai profité des variantes que m'offroient quelquefois ces différens manuscrits, et j'en ai augmenté mon texte" (I, vj). He supplied no notes or variants.

From about 1830 on, editors took more seriously the archival aspect of their work. Excited by the discovery of new manuscripts, they gave complete references, often with descriptions, for the manuscripts they had consulted and indicated precisely which manuscript had been followed as the base for the edition and which one(s) had furnished variants. For example, the *Supplément, variantes et corrections* published by Polycarpe Chabaille (Paris, 1835) to accompany Méon's *Renart* edition provided considerable information about the manuscripts Méon had used, and Chabaille took care to reproduce variant readings exactly as they appeared in the manuscripts: "Quelques fautes évidentes échappées aux scribes ont été relevées, mais en prenant la précaution de renfermer entre crochets [ ] les corrections proposées, en sorte qu'il sera facile de les reconnoître et de les adopter ou de les rejeter" (xxii).

One of the most gifted and indefatigable editors of this period was Francisque Michel (1809–87), best known perhaps for his *editio princeps* of the Oxford manuscript of the *Chanson de Roland* (Paris, 1837). In editions involving two manuscripts, such as the *Lai de l'Ombre* (in *Lais inédits des XIIᵉ et XIIIᵉ siècles* [Paris, 1836]), Gerbert de Montreuil's *Roman de la Violette* (Paris, 1834), and the *Mémoires de Jean, sire de Joinville* (Paris, 1830; rpt. 1858), Michel selected the better manuscript as the base of his text and followed it quite closely; he corrected some errors and omissions, either from the second manuscript or from context, and supplied important variants from the second manuscript in an appendix or at the bottom of the page. His choice of the basic manuscript was a subjective decision, taking into account its age, quality, completeness, and other characteristics; similarly, the location of errors and omissions in the text and the use of variants to correct these errors depended on the editor's knowledge of manuscripts and Old French and on his flair. Each problem required a separate, individual solution. Michel had excellent flair, but he worked independently and never tried to formulate rules for handling texts.[4]

During the 1850s an attempt was made to refine these empirical procedures for teaching purposes and for use in a series of editions sponsored by the French government and directed by Francis Guessard, professor at the Ecole des chartes, the French national school which had been established in 1821 to train scholars and librarians in the handling of manuscripts and documents. According to an imperial decree of February 12, 1856, the "Anciens Poëtes de la France" collection was to comprise forty volumes, encompassing almost all genres of Old French literature from the epic to the *Roman de la Rose*; however, only the first ten volumes appeared, between 1858 and 1870, containing fourteen epics.[5]

The editorial policy of the entire series was summarized enthusiastically by Léon Gautier, a student of Guessard's, in *Les Epopées françaises* (1st ed.; Paris, 1865; I, 186–91). For

---

[4] See William Roach, "Francisque Michel: A Pioneer in Medieval Studies," *Proceedings of the American Philosophical Society*, 114 (1970), 168–78. In an appendix Roach lists Michel's principal editions and other writings.

[5] Vol. 1, *Gui de Bourgogne, Otinel, Floovant*, ed. Guessard and H. Michelant (1858); vol. 2, *Doon de Mayence*, ed. A. Pey (1859); vol. 3, *Gaufrey*, ed. Guessard and P. Chabaille (1859); vol. 4, *Fierabras*, ed. A. Kroeber and G. Servois, and *Parise la Duchesse*, ed. Guessard and L. Larchey (1860); vol. 5, *Huon de Bordeaux*, ed. Guessard and C. Grandmaison (1860); vol. 6, *Aye d'Avignon*, ed. Guessard and P. Meyer, and *Gui de Nanteuil*, ed. P. Meyer (1861); vol. 7, *Gaydon*, ed. Guessard and S. Luce (1862); vol. 8, *Hugues Capet*, ed. Le Marquis de la Grange (1864); vol. 9, *Macaire*, ed. Guessard (1866); vol. 10, *Aliscans*, ed. Guessard and A. de Montaiglon (1870). These editions were reprinted in 1966.

A planning report submitted by H. Fortoul, Minister of Public Instruction, prompted the imperial decree. A sample edition of the first 1800 lines of the *Chanson d'Aspremont* published by Guessard and Gautier in 1855 supported the report, but was never completed; Gautier's *Bibliographie des chansons de geste* (Paris, 1897) described the twenty-four-page pamphlet as "rarissime" (59). Fortoul's report and the beginning of Napoléon III's decree were reprinted in *BEC*, 17 (1856), 297–99. See also the Prospectus circulated by the original publisher, P. Jannet, reproduced in *BEC*, 19 (1858), 211–15, and the announcement of the transfer of the series to a new publisher, A. Franck, in *BEC*, 21 (1860), 197.

every poem, the editor was to publish the oldest version in its entirety. Should this version be judged incomplete or defective, "on devait en combler les lacunes et en corriger les fautes avec les plus respectables des autres manuscrits que l'on aurait eu préalablement le soin de classer dans l'ordre de leur importance et de leur ancienneté. Mais, en ce cas, on devait indiquer à l'aide de certains signes typographiques, que tel ou tel passage était emprunté à tel ou tel manuscrit, et non plus à celui que l'on prenait pour base de la publication" (187f.). To make the extent of the editor's intervention absolutely clear, the introduction to each epic includes a detailed explanation of how its text was established.

What ought to be the editor's responsibility, in the series, to the letter of his basic manuscript? During the 1850s this issue aroused a lively controversy between French medievalists—trained at the Ecole des chartes to respect documents—and classicists. Should the editor reproduce his text as it stood in the manuscript, or should he try to recast it into the "classical" Francien literary dialect, as editors of Latin texts attempted to restore the classical literary language written by Cicero and Lucan? Guessard took the conservative position of preserving scrupulously the readings of the basic manuscript, as Gautier reported: "Il fut décidé que l'on aurait la religion de nos manuscrits, sans toutefois en avoir la superstition; que les textes en seraient toujours reproduits avec exactitude, quel que fût d'ailleurs leur dialecte, et qu'enfin on ne se résoudrait à les corriger que dans les cas assez rares où il y aurait une évidente incorrection due à la sottise ou à la légèreté des scribes" (189).

In practice, the editors working with Guessard put all editorial emendations and all borrowings from other manuscripts in square brackets; they usually justified any departure from the basic manuscript in a note, and they provided a selection of variants where more than one manuscript was involved. They experimented with various techniques for handling disparities which arose when the manuscript supplying corrections featured a different dialect from the basic manuscript. For *Otinel*, Guessard and Michelant filled in the gaps of the basic manuscript, written in continental Old French, with passages taken from an Anglo-Norman manuscript; they apologized for the "fâcheuse bigarrure" which resulted from their scrupulous fidelity to the manuscripts. But for *Huon de Bordeaux*, Guessard and Grandmaison modified the borrowed passages to conform to the dialect and orthography of the basic manuscript; they enclosed these passages in brackets and warned philologists bent on dialect study to take their examples from elsewhere in the text. In a more daring venture, for *Macaire*, Guessard printed on facing pages a faithful transcription of the unique manuscript, which presents a Franco-Venetian redaction, and his own reconstruction of the Francien text which, he believed, had served as the Italian *remanieur*'s model.

The editions in the "Anciens Poëtes de la France" series are then characterized by assessments of manuscript quality which determine the basic manuscript, systematic respect for the text of a single basic manuscript, scrupulous typographical indication of each departure from this manuscript, and notes giving the reasons for those departures—features which foreshadow the post-1913 practices of the Bédierist school. Except in cases where the discovery of additional manuscripts has rendered them unsatisfactory, the editions remain valuable today; in a recent study of *Gaydon*, for example, Jean Subrenat terms the edition established by Guessard and Luce correct and "irremplaçable."[6] On the other hand, it should be remembered that Gautier, even in 1865, viewed these editions merely as intermediate stages in the process of achieving purified texts, closer to the poet's original; the ultimate goal was to publish "des éditions classiques, 'en bon français'" (191). In addition, the series had almost no influence on the next period of Old French editions. It received favorable reviews in its early years;[7] but by 1866, recent advances in German scholarship, heralded as the achievement of a truly scientific method, were fomenting a revolution in Old French editing. Soon a new method, which

---

[6] *Etude sur Gaydon, chanson de geste du XIIIᵉ siècle* (Etudes littéraires, 1; Univ. de Provence, 1974), p. 14.

[7] See the review of vols. 1–5 by H. d'Arbois de Jubainville in *BEC*, 23 (1862), 362–65; also his review of vol. 9 (*Macaire*), *BEC*, 28 (1867), 480–83. Laudatory reviews of a few volumes appear in the *Journal des Savants*: e.g., vol. 4, juin 1860, pp. 388–89; vol. 8, juin 1864, p. 390, and février 1865, pp. 88–105.

would dominate the field for a half-century, triumphed over the old school. Exemplary though they seem today, the "Anciens Poëtes de la France" editions, along with the other less systematic but often admirable products of the empirical period, rapidly became obsolete.

III. THE SCIENTIFIC PERIOD

Pioneering French proponents of the new method for editing Old French texts called it "the scientific method" or "the method for classifying manuscripts." Today it is frequently termed "the method of common error" or "the Lachmann method," after the German scholar who gave it definitive form.[8] This method originated in the work of various eighteenth-century German classical philologists editing the Greek New Testament, notably J. A. Bengel, J. J. Wettstein, J. S. Semler, and J. J. Griesbach. Karl Lachmann (1793–1851) refined it further to reduce the role of the editor's subjective judgment and applied it to several texts, including the New Testament, Lucretius's *De Rerum Natura*, and medieval German poems. By dint of his personality and authoritative critical prefaces, Lachmann founded a school.

Underlying this method is a different critical attitude towards the work of medieval scribes and authors. The empirical editors had attempted to understand and repair errors committed by scribes, especially those which produced an incomplete or incoherent text. They tried to improve the text of the best manuscript available to them, but they rarely ventured to restore the text to the form it had borne on leaving the author's hands. In fact, the author's holograph for Old French texts has virtually always disappeared, so for all practical purposes any

---

[8] Was Bédier responsible for introducing the phrase to France? See his references to Lachmann as inventor of the method in his 1913 edition of the *Lai de l'Ombre* (SATF), xxiii, xli. The real contributions to the method of Lachmann and his predecessors are delineated by Sebastiano Timpanaro, *La genesi del metodo del Lachmann* (Florence, 1963).

reference to the original or archetype of existing copies denotes a hypothetical approximation of that original. Reconstructing this hypothetical ancestor was precisely the goal of the new method, which emphasized the author's literary creation and valued any manuscripts only as means to attaining the lost model of which all surviving manuscripts were presumed to represent imperfect or intentionally revised copies. Another essential aspect of the new method was the systematization of the editor's work, a reaction against what were seen as the haphazard practices of the empirical school and the real shortcomings of some of its products. The younger generation of French scholars criticized their predecessors for making subjective choices of a "best manuscript," for arbitrarily deciding that a particular reading had resulted from a scribal error, and for correcting the error with a variant selected for vague, willful, or unscientific reasons. The cure for the unrestricted application of subjective judgment to textual problems was to be an objective, rational method which any conscientious editor might apply rigorously.

Two stages characterize the new method: one concerned with discovering which readings are authentic, i.e., derive from the author; the other, with clothing these readings in the language presumably written by the author. Where several manuscripts of a work survive, the editor must begin by classifying them, that is, determining their relationships to each other and to the hypothetical original. The common error is the basis of this classification: if a group of manuscripts shares significant errors which cannot have been committed independently by their various scribes, the manuscripts must be descendants of the same model and therefore constitute a family. Once the relationships of the families have been determined and diagrammed in a *stemma codicum* (genealogical tree of the manuscripts), the editor may proceed to reconstruct the original text. If there are three families, the original is determined automatically by the agreement of two of them; if there are only two families, or if each of the three families has a different reading, the editor must rely on other sources or his own judgment to choose the original. The text resulting from this method might be based on a single manuscript which is not too far down the genealogical tree from the original, with emendations wherever the agreement of the other families shows it to be idiosyncratic, but the final edition is more usually a composite of readings thought to be authentic. In the second stage, the editor rewrites this composite text to make it conform to the author's own language—where that may be determined—in morphology, phonology, syntax, and dialect, which no manuscript preserves perfectly. The final product is called a "critical text."

The most active and influential advocate for the scientific method in France was the young Gaston Paris (1839–1903), seconded vigorously, at least in the transitional period between 1866 and 1875, by Paul Meyer (1840–1917). They had become friends during their student days at the Ecole des chartes, where, like Gautier, they had taken courses with Guessard. According to Meyer,[9] he and Paris first encountered the method for manuscript classification in Karl Bartsch's edition of *Das Nibelungenlied* (Leipzig, 1866), which Paris reviewed for the *Revue critique d'histoire et de littérature* (22 septembre 1866, pp. 183–89), a journal which they had founded that same year, with Charles Morel and Hermann Suchier, for the purpose of analyzing scholarly work and propagating new rigorous methods for historical research.[10]

Together Paris and Meyer waged an energetic campaign to convert other scholars to scientific textual criticism. On the rear, they disparaged editions produced by the empirical method;[11] in the vanguard, they encouraged the classification of

---

[9] "M. Gustav Gröber" [necrology], *Romania*, 40 (1911), 632 n 2.

[10] See the journal's Prospectus, reprinted in *BEC*, 27 (1866), 190f.

[11] See, for example, Meyer's review of Chrétien's *Perceval le Gallois*, ed. Charles Potvin (Mons, 1865), in *Revue critique*, 1er septembre 1866, pp. 129–37; Bartsch's review of Gautier, *Les Epopées françaises*, vol. I (Paris, 1865), in *Revue critique*, 29 décembre 1866, pp. 406–14; Meyer's joint review of *La Conquête de Jérusalem*, ed. C. Hippeau (Paris, 1868), and *La Chanson de Roland et le Roman de Roncevaux des XIIe et XIIIe siècles*, ed. F. Michel (Paris, 1869), in *BEC*, 31 (1870), 227–33. Meyer attacked Michel with particular force, accusing him of having remained "étranger au mouvement philologique de ces dernières années" and concluding: "il est pénible en effet d'avoir à constater qu'une œuvre aussi faible est sortie de la plume d'un savant qui a rendu autrefois de si nombreux services à la philologie française." Michel's *Roland* was rehabilitated by Bédier in his long article on *Roland* editions in *Romania* (1937–38).

manuscripts and the publication of critical texts, and they taught the new method to budding philologists. In still another sector of their campaign, they established a journal and a series of editions to publish the new scholarship about medieval texts. *Romania*, founded in 1872, was to promulgate learned articles and editions of short works; the Société des Anciens Textes Français, started in 1875, aimed to sponsor editions of longer works at reasonable prices.

In the *Revue critique* (21 août 1869, pp. 121–26), Paris hailed Gustav Gröber's work on *Fierabras* as the first attempt to classify the manuscripts of an Old French epic; though he did not entirely agree with Gröber's results, he found the German scholar's critical method superior to the "vague and arbitrary" handling of manuscripts by the "Anciens Poëtes de la France" editors of *Fierabras*. As early as 1868, Paris was classifying the manuscripts of the *Vie de saint Alexis* with his students at the Ecole des Hautes Etudes, in preparation for his edition of 1872.[12] Meyer classified the manuscripts of *Girart de Roussillon* at about the same time (*Jahrbuch für romanische und englische Literatur*, 11 [1870], 121–42).

The first two Old French editions published according to the scientific method triumphantly broke new ground in editing practice: Natalis de Wailly's critical text of Joinville's *Histoire de saint Louis* in 1868 and Paris's *Vie de saint Alexis* four years later. Wailly had started by trying to reconstruct Joinville's original dictated text from later faulty copies; Joinville's own manuscript and even the illuminated codex presented to Louis le Hutin in 1309 had been lost. Wailly classified the three extant manuscripts, seeing *A* (Paris, B.N. fr. 13568) as a copy of the presentation manuscript and the other two manuscripts as copies of Joinville's personal draft, and he published a composite text based on *A* in 1867. At that time he thought that it would be impossible to restore Joinville's thirteenth-century forms to the text "sans risquer de le dénaturer par des corrections systématiques." However, by 1867, the new method was

---

[12] Meyer, *Romania*, 40 (1911), 632; *Vie de saint Alexis*, ed. Gaston Paris and Léopold Pannier (BÉHÉ; Paris, 1872), p. v. Pannier edited the fourteenth-century text.

in vogue, and Wailly's reviewers urged him to "vieillir la langue du ms."[13] After studying legal documents from the Join-ville chancellery, Wailly felt competent to impose thirteenth-century Champenois forms on his text for a new edition in 1868 (Société de l'Histoire de France, 144). The revised *editio maior*, which appeared in 1874, elicited Gaston Paris's praise for its application of "la méthode, seule vraiment scientifique, de la classification des manuscrits." However, Paris disagreed with Wailly's stemma and also contended that the editor had not gone far enough in regularizing *A*'s orthography: he charged Wailly with "respect exagéré pour le manuscrit"![14] Yet Wailly had imposed approximately five thousand alterations on the text of his basic manuscript. (We should point out here that in reviews of critical texts debates over stemmas and de-tails of language reconstruction are not uncommon; the method invites constant tinkering and revision in these areas.)

As a trend-setter, Paris's edition of the *Alexis* was more influential than Wailly's Joinville text, though it appeared later. Its significance is due in part to a long preface (138 pages) in which Paris explained and demonstrated each aspect of the critical method and urged its use, even as he admitted its lim-itation: it could never produce the genuine original, merely a possible text of the original (12f.). From four *Alexis* manu-scripts of the twelfth and thirteenth centuries, Paris recon-structed an archetype to which he assigned the year 1040 as its probable date of composition; it was couched in an ancient literary language which he thought predated the divergence of Francien and Norman into separate dialects. He considered his text valuable not only as the earliest version of the *Alexis*, but also as a specimen of "la bonne langue française telle qu'elle devait se parler et s'écrire au milieu du XIe siècle" (135), a linguistic stage which no literary manuscript had preserved.

---

[13] Meyer, in *Revue critique*, 9 février 1867, p. 90; see also H. d'Arbois de Jubainville, in *BEC*, 28 (1867), 400–03. Only eight years earlier Arbois de Jubainville had waxed ecstatic over F. Michel's Joinville edition, which repro-duced manuscript *A* quite faithfully; see *BEC*, 20 (1859), 534–36.

[14] *Romania*, 3 (1874), 401–13; see Wailly's reply in *Romania*, 3, 487–93. Wailly's stemma is no longer accepted; see Noel L. Corbett, ed., *La Vie de saint Louis* (Sherbrooke, Quebec, 1977), pp. 17–39.

In later editions Paris modified various details in an attempt to restore this language more accurately.

To illustrate the extent to which a critical text established by a committed scientific editor may depart from the text preserved in the extant manuscripts, let us contrast the various versions of the first stanza of the *Vie de saint Alexis*. The texts of three of the four manuscripts known to Gaston Paris, plus variants from the fourth, are transcribed below from the diplomatic edition in the *Altfranzösisches Übungsbuch*, edited by W. Foerster and E. Koschwitz (4th ed.; Leipzig, 1911). Words have been separated and abbreviations resolved, but no punctuation has been added.

Manuscripts *L* (Hildesheim, formerly Lamspringe) and *A* (Ashburnham) were copied in the twelfth century in England; although they are the oldest manuscripts, they are considerably more recent than the eleventh-century date of composition usually ascribed to the poem, and both are strongly marked by Anglo-Norman traits. *P* (Paris, B.N. fr. 19525) and *S* (Paris, B.N. fr. 12471) are thirteenth-century manuscripts copied in France. According to Paris's 1872 stemma, these manuscripts group themselves into two families, *LA* and *PS*; both families probably derive from a faulty copy of the original, rather than the original itself. *L* is the closest descendant of the original, being separated from it by only two hypothetical intermediaries, so it was considered the most exact reflection of the original in content and form, even though its Anglo-Norman dialect, according to Paris, disguises the original's pure Francien language.

L

Bons fut li secles al tens ancienur
quer feit i ert e justise ed amur
s'i ert creance dunt ore n'i at nul prut
tut est muez perdut ad sa colur
ja mais n'iert tel cum fut as anceisurs

A

Bons fu li siecles al tens ancienur
kar feis i ert e justise e amur
s'i iert creance dunt or n'i ad . . .
tut est muez perdu ad sa culur
ja mais n'ier tel cum fu as ancessur(s)

According to Paris, the *A* scribe wrote *nul pru* at the end of the third line, which the medieval corrector changed to *udur.* The *Übungsbuch* omits these words.

S is equivalent to *A* in substance, except for the following variants:

> 3 or n'i a mais prou—4 si est m. perdue a sa valour—
> 5 *lacking.*

P

Bons fu li siecles al tens ancienor
car feiz ert et justise et amor
s'i ert creance dunt or n'i a nul pro
tot est muez perdu a sa color
ja mais n'iert tel cum fu as anchesors

Now compare these texts with two different critical reconstructions by Paris, his first effort of 1872 and a later revised version (Paris, 1903; rev. ed., CFMA, 1911):

1872

Bons fut li siecles al tens ancienor,
Quer feit i ert e justise et amor,
Si ert credance, dont or n'i at nul prot:
Tot est mudez, perdude at sa color;
Ja mais n'iert tels com fut as anceisors.

1903

Bons fuṭ li siecleṣ al tems ancienour,
Quer feiṭ i ereṭ e justisie eḍ amour,
S'i ert creḍance, dont or n'i aṭ nul prouṭ;
Toz est muḍez, perduḍe aṭ sa colour:
Ja mais n'iert tels com fuṭ as anceisours.

Within ten years the method of common error was firmly established in Old French editing circles. It provided the theoretical basis for the majority of all editions of Old French works represented in three or more manuscripts. Two outstanding monuments to the method and to sheer perseverance on the editor's part are Léopold Constans's edition of *Le Roman de Thèbes* (2 vols.; SATF; Paris, 1890) and Edmund Stengel's critical text, *Das altfranzösische Rolandslied* (vol. I, Kritische Ausgabe; Leipzig, 1900).[15]

Constans, a student of Gaston Paris, classified the five complete *Thèbes* manuscripts into four families: *S*, *CB*, *A*, and *P*. *C*, *A*, and *P* date from the thirteenth century; *B* and *S*, from the fourteenth. However, Constans felt that the late Anglo-Norman *S* reproduced the archetype more faithfully than the others because it was copied in England, a linguistically conservative area, and preserved traits of the western French dialect in which the original was composed. Reasoning thus, he made *S* his basic manuscript, but he eliminated many passages he deemed interpolations by the *S*-redactor and added passages when the other manuscripts were united against *S*, with the result that the substance of Constans's 10,230-line romance does not correspond to what appears in any extant manuscript: *A* contains 14,626 lines; *B*, 10,541; *C*, 10,562; *P*, 13,296; *S*, 11,546. Moreover, the language of the critical text represents Constans's reconstruction of the language of *S*'s model, a manuscript he thought written in the west or northwest of France during the twelfth century. Although Paul Meyer, in his review, admired Constans's assiduity, he wondered whether this critical text was worth the tedious labor it had exacted; if *S* does not merit the high stemmatic position that Constans granted it, "toute l'édition s'écroule" (108). Recently Guy Raynaud de Lage stressed that "l'édition de Constans est en réalité une nouvelle version, une cinquième version du roman" (ix).

Stengel worked from a stemma, now rejected, which divided the *Roland* representatives into four families: OV^4, V^7CPLT, n, and k.[16] Here *O* had the same value as V^4, and

---

[15] On *Thèbes*, see Constans's Introduction in vol. II; also Meyer's review in *Romania*, 21 (1892), 107–09, and Guy Raynaud de Lage's Introduction to his edition of *Thèbes* (2 vols.; CFMA; Paris, 1966–68). On Stengel's *Roland* text, see the second and third parts of Bédier's evaluation of *Roland* editions; also Whitehead, "The Textual Criticism of the *Chanson de Roland*."

[16] *O* and V^4 contain assonanced Old French texts, while CV^7PLT offer rhymed versions, also in Old French. *K* stands for the *Ruolandes liet* by the Bavarian priest Konrad; n, for the Norwegian redaction, branch VIII of the *Karlamagnussaga*. O = Oxford, Bodleian Library, Digby 23; V^4 = Venice, Biblioteca Marciana 225 (formerly fr. IV); C = Châteauroux, Bibl. munic. 1; V^7 = Venice, Biblioteca Marciana 251 (formerly fr. VII); P = Paris, B.N. fr. 860; L = Lyon, Bibl. de la Ville 984; T = Cambridge, Trinity College R 3–32.

together the assonanced O and V^4 had no more weight than the rhymed representatives V^7CPLT. Taking O as his base, Stengel constructed a composite archetype which added 637 lines to O's 3,998 lines, and he rewrote about 1,000 more lines on the authority of the other witnesses; he also replaced O's Anglo-Norman dialect with Francien forms. Whitehead described the Stengel edition as "essentially a conflation of the terse Digby version with the prolix rhymed *remaniement*—a mixture, that is to say, of two different works each with its own distinctive character" (81). At the turn of the century, confidence in the method of common error was a mighty boon when editors had to distinguish between lacunas and interpolations, between authentic forms and scribal mistakes.

Throughout this period, however, there were reservations about the method, as well as technical disagreements about its implementation. Early on, Meyer doubted that it could be used with an assonanced *chanson de geste*,[17] and Gautier later emphasized the necessity for honoring the basic manuscript of an epic when its readings were equivalent to other variants, rather than making a choice on the basis of taste, as Paris recommended.[18] At the end of a generally favorable review of the *Alexis* edition, Henry Nicol called attention to the disadvantages of Paris's method. He felt that Paris had underrated both the importance of a faithful transcription of the best manuscript(s) of a work and the danger of the reader's accepting the editor's conclusions too hastily: "Instead of having first a true copy of the document which is the most important part of the evidence, and then having what the editor believes—in the main, no doubt, on sufficient grounds—to have been its original form, we are always prejudiced (I use the word in its etymological sense) by the editor's opinion." Nicol also questioned the value of critical texts for works such as translations, whose interest is mainly linguistic.[19]

---

[17] Review of Potvin's *Perceval*, *Revue critique*, 1er septembre 1866, p. 129.

[18] *Les Epopees françaises*, 2nd ed. (Paris, 1878), I, 262f. Gautier's editions of the *Roland* seem to move reluctantly towards a thoroughly reconstructed composite text.

[19] "An Account of M. Gaston Paris's Method of Editing in his *Vie de saint Alexis*," in *Transactions of the Philological Society*, 1873–74, pp. 332–45.

Meyer himself, in a report to the Philological Society of London on the achievements of Romance philology between 1870 and 1874, expressed misgivings about the language reconstruction required to restore a text to its original form. He drew a distinction between the privileged situation of Joinville's text, where the author's dictation was presumably written down by the same scribe(s) who transcribed official documents in Joinville's chancellery, and the more common problem presented by Villehardouin's chronicle, for which the author's exact language could not be determined. In the first case, Wailly was fully justified in modifying the language of his basic manuscript to make it conform to that of the Joinville charters; in the latter, Wailly was wise to adhere more closely to his basic manuscript. Paris's *Alexis* edition, declared Meyer, exceeded the limit of scholarly certainty; rather than being taken as a model, it must be regarded as a scientific experiment: "C'est là un cas tout à fait à part, qui peut être admis à titre d'expérience scientifique. Hors de là, il y a un inconvénient évident à franchir la limite qui sépare le domaine des faits de celui des conjectures." Meyer particularly opposed the orthographical regularization of the *Alexis*, and he feared that, in the hands of imprudent editors, such techniques for altering the text of manuscripts could lead to ridiculous ends. By contrast, he commented favorably on Paris's side-by-side presentation of the manuscript text and his critical reconstruction of the original for the *Vie de saint Léger* (*Romania*, 1 [1872], 273–317), which exists in a unique manuscript. Here, as Nicol urged, the reader can evaluate the editor's conclusions for himself.[20]

In his own work, henceforth Meyer opted for "le domaine des faits," leaving the conjectures, more and more, to Gaston Paris.[21] He never completed the edition of *Girart de Roussillon*

---

[20] "Rapport de M. Paul Meyer sur les progrès de la philologie romane," in *Transactions of the Philological Society*, 1873–74, pp. 407–39; rpt. in *BEC*, 35 (1874), 631–54.

[21] See the vignettes of Guessard, Meyer, Paris, and Gautier in Maurice Prou's centennial history of the Ecole des chartes, *Livre du centenaire (1821– 1921)*, vol. I, *L'Ecole: son histoire, son œuvre* (Paris, 1921), pp. xxviii, xli–xlii, cxxvii–cxxxv.

for which he had classified the manuscripts; and, although he edited numerous other texts, he seems to have avoided cases which required the use or rejection of the common error method.

A few other editors found the method unsuitable to the textual tradition with which they were working. For example, Gaston Raynaud described the preparation of his edition of *La Châtelaine de Vergy* from nine thirteenth- and fourteenth-century manuscripts in terms reminiscent of the empirical period: "Ces manuscrits n'étant pas susceptibles d'un classement rigoureux, nous avons dû nous contenter de reproduire l'un d'eux, le ms. *C*, que nous avons, à l'occasion, corrigé et amélioré par la comparaison avec les autres."[22] Though Wendelin Foerster never explained just how he constructed his composite texts of Chrétien de Troyes's romances, he, too, seems to have preferred an empirical approach to the rigid application of the common error method—or at least an idiosyncratic combination of the two methods, since he did restore a Champenois dialect to the romances. Most important for the future of editing techniques, the young Joseph Bédier (1864–1938) appeared to harbor doubts about his classification of the manuscripts of the *Lai de l'Ombre* before the turn of the century: "Ces six manuscrits me *paraissent* se grouper trois à trois en deux familles: *ABC, DEF*" (Fribourg, 1890; p. 14, emphasis ours); nevertheless, he constructed a composite text from his stemma in the customary way and regularized the orthography of the poem. Gaston Paris promptly disagreed with Bédier's classification, arguing for a three-family stemma: "Il résulte de ces remarques que bien probablement le lai de l'*Ombre* nous est conservé non par deux, mais par trois familles, *y* [= *AB C*], *v* [= *DF*], *E*, et que par conséquent l'original commun se reconstitue, à coup sûr, par l'accord de *y* ou de *v* ensemble ou avec *E*" (*Romania*, 19 [1890], 611). When Bédier returned to the *Lai de l'Ombre* twenty years later, he was to react against the com-

---

[22] Introduction (CFMA; Paris, 1910), p. v.; this volume contains a revised version of the text printed in *Romania*, 21 (1892), 145–93. In the Introduction to his 1913 edition of the *Lai de l'Ombre*, Bédier viewed Meyer, Raynaud, and Auguste Longnon (editor of François Villon's poems) as forerunners (p. xli).

mon error method as strenuously as his mentor, Gaston Paris, had reacted against the empirical school.

IV. CRISIS OF CONFIDENCE

In 1913 Bédier published a new edition of the *Lai de l'Ombre* (SATF), which, together with its Introduction, opened an unstable new period in editing Old French texts, for Bédier rejected what he began calling the Lachmann method, both in practice and in theory. Instead, he urged a more modest role for the editor, a role similar to that played by the best of the empirical editors.

Made uneasy by Gaston Paris's criticism of his 1890 stemma for the poem, Bédier examined stemmas established by other Old French editors and discovered a "loi surprenante": in seventy-eight out of eighty cases, the stemmas had two main branches or families; three-branch stemmas were rare in editions. This meant in practice that whenever the two families disagreed, the editor reconstructing their archetype had to choose between them; he thus enjoyed a measure of latitude for exercising his critical judgment. By contrast, a significant number of the stemmas proposed by reviewers or scholars who classified manuscripts without editing them had three branches. Therefore, Bédier concluded, the Lachmann method of manuscript classification must be fundamentally flawed because it allows editors to manipulate their variant distribution in order to obtain stemmas giving them the greatest possible freedom in establishing their texts. Any such manipulation, thought Bédier, arises from the editor's unconscious desire to control his edition, rather than a lack of principles. Hence, the method, not the editor, must be at fault.

Having disputed the objectivity and validity of the Lachmann method, Bédier went on to examine the particular case of the *Lai de l'Ombre*. In addition to the two stemmas proposed in 1890, he drew up two more which provided equally probable explanations of the poem's variant distribution; three others could also be sketched, he claimed. Each stemma would, of course, require the constitution of a different critical text. It became clear, then, that no stemma was certain. Instead of creating an artificial composite monster, Bédier preferred to stick to what was genuine in a documentary sense: a manuscript. Thus, he edited the *Lai de l'Ombre* as it appeared in manuscript *A* (Paris, B.N. fr. 837), chosen because it offers a coherent text and needs few emendations. To correct scribal errors, Bédier intervened 34 times in 962 lines, justifying each correction in the notes to the text: "Nous avons tâché de collaborer avec Jean Renart le moins possible. Nous n'offrons au lecteur rien que le texte d'un bon manuscrit, réparé seulement dans les quelques cas ci-dessus énumérés. L'archéologue Didron a dit un jour cette sage parole: 'Il faut conserver le plus possible, réparer le moins possible, ne restaurer à aucun prix'. Ce qu'il disait des vieilles pierres doit s'entendre aussi, croyons-nous, de nos beaux vieux textes" (xlv).[23]

Not long after Bédier's challenge to the Lachmann procedures for manuscript classification came an attempt to refine the method by making it more objective and "scientific" and capable of handling large numbers of manuscripts. Dom Henri Quentin, a member of a commission assigned by the Vatican to edit the Vulgate, described his new method first in *Mémoire sur l'établissement du texte de la Vulgate* (Rome, 1922) and then defended it in *Essais de critique textuelle* (Paris, 1926), where he responded to critics' negative reviews.

Dom Quentin brought two modifications to the Lachmann method. One concerned the concept of common error, which he thought led to a vicious circle because the editor labeled as an error something which he thought could not have figured in the archetype; yet he could not construct the archetype until after he had classified the manuscripts, so his identification of

---

[23] Note that even the analogy which Bédier draws between textual criticism and archeology is a reaction against Gaston Paris, who compared the modernizations inflicted on medieval texts by scribal *remanieurs* with the structural renovations suffered by Romanesque churches: "J'ai essayé de faire ici pour la langue française ce que ferait un architecte qui voudrait reconstruire sur le papier Saint-Germain des Prés tel que l'admira le XIe siècle" (*Alexis*, p. 136).

errors depended on his preconceptions about the archetype. Dom Quentin preferred to replace the common error with the neutral category of variant, which implies no assumptions about the archetype. His second innovation was a procedure for determining the relationships among manuscripts: by comparing the variants from selected passages of three manuscripts at a time according to rather complicated charts and computations, the editor may discover whether one manuscript is the intermediary between the other two. For instance, if this procedure indicates that a manuscript C is intermediate between B and D, any of the following stemmas is possible:

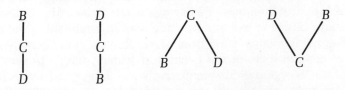

When all the intermediaries have been identified, the editor may establish the correct stemma by examining the intrinsic value of the individual variants, the history of the manuscripts, and the rest of the classification. Thus, the sorting by threes is intended to refine the early stages of classification by making it computational rather than judgmental; the rest of the process follows standard Lachmann techniques, using even the concept of error. Once the stemma is established, it allows the editor to construct the archetype with confidence: "Le canon critique pour l'établissement du texte se cueille comme un fruit mûr sur le schéma généalogique une fois que celui-ci a pris sa forme définitive" (*Essais*, 90).

To prove the efficacy of his technique, which had already enabled his team of collaborators to produce an edition of the Octateuch based on seventy manuscripts classified into a three-branch stemma, Dom Quentin tackled several other reportedly recalcitrant traditions, among them the *Lai de l'Ombre*. Here, using the variants from a sample of sixty-eight lines, he constructed a new stemma which he considered valid for determining the poem's archetype. This fifth stemma would supersede the four previous ones published by Bédier and Paris.

According to Dom Quentin, the circular concept of common error had prevented Bédier from classifying the *Lai* manuscripts accurately.

Bédier wasted no time in joining the fray with a witty polemical reply, "La tradition manuscrite du *Lai de l'Ombre*: réflexions sur l'art d'éditer les anciens textes," in *Romania*, 1928. Here he developed the two major arguments of his 1913 Préface: the predominance of two-branch stemmas signals a fatal flaw in the Lachmann system for manuscript classification; and the various stemmas possible for the *Lai de l'Ombre* prove that any composite reconstruction is only a hypothesis, an intellectual game. As a cause of the surprising prevalence of bipartite stemmas, Bédier again cited the editor's unconscious desire to exercise his judgment in establishing the text. Following a suggestion from Mario Roques, he added another factor—the logic of the Lachmann system, which pushes the editor to organize his manuscripts into larger and larger families until at last all are classified into two irreconcilable groups. Disenchanted with composite texts, Bédier again urged "un retour vers la technique des anciens humanistes" (177). Then he examined Dom Quentin's method and his stemma for the *Lai de l'Ombre*, rejecting both. He questioned the validity of basing any stemma on such a small textual sample and found the archetype constructed according to the Benedictine's stemma generally unsatisfactory on literary grounds. Bédier concluded that, while Dom Quentin's techniques work in Old French for determining family groups, if not the higher relationships of the families, they offer nothing really new or helpful. When all Lachmann methods have been proved deficient, the editor must place his trust in the manuscript and in his own judgment, risky as that may be:

> Aussi la méthode d'édition la plus recommandable est-elle peut-être, en dernière analyse, celle que régit un esprit de défiance de soi, de prudence, d'extrême 'conservatisme', un énergique vouloir, porté jusqu'au parti pris, d'ouvrir aux scribes le plus large crédit et de ne toucher au texte d'un manuscrit que l'on imprime qu'en cas d'extrême et presque évidente nécessité: toutes les corrections conjecturales devraient être reléguées en quelque appendice. [356]

The Bédier–Dom Quentin controversy provoked a spate of articles on editing which has yet to subside. Questions raised by the two scholars about the Lachmann method threatened the theoretical foundations of textual criticism not only in Old French, but also in classics, where the common error method had developed and still reigned supreme, and in other modern languages, especially Italian. The ensuing debate produced a period of uncertainty about editing premises in Old French that is still not entirely resolved; on the positive side, it has paved the way for some experiments with new procedures and for a thoughtful reassessment of the editor's role and goals. The possible emergence of a new consensus will be the subject of Chapter V; here we shall trace the main currents of the storm stirred up by Bédier and Dom Quentin.

In *La Critique des textes* (Paris, 1931), the classicist Paul Collomp started out to defend the traditional Lachmann method against the recent criticisms from both ends of the spectrum, but he ended by simply stating its limits: one can seldom succeed in constructing a stemma where the manuscript tradition is contaminated; even if a plausible stemma can be established in such a case, the text reconstituted from it will be uncertain. Nevertheless, Collomp was not sure that Bédier had invalidated the common error method in simpler cases (pp. i–iii, 65–72).

Bédier's position won support from many scholars versed in the transmission problems of Old French texts, but with various misgivings. An unusual, if understandable, injection of overt postwar nationalism into the academic debate came from a Belgian, Maurice Wilmotte, who hailed the Frenchman's rejection of the positivistic method originally developed by Germans ("Sur la critique des textes," in *Etudes de philologie wallonne* [Paris, 1932; first published in *Le Correspondant*, 10 mai 1920], pp. 3–38). M. Dominica Legge, in "Recent Methods of Textual Criticism" (*Arthuriana*, 2 [1929–30], 48–55), welcomed the end of language reconstruction and the de-dialectizing of basic manuscripts; she approved Bédier's conservatism as "the safest course" for the time being. In a more emotional vein, P. S. Coculesco endorsed all of Bédier's arguments, while condemning both Dom Quentin's method and the Lachmann system ("Sur les méthodes de critique textuelle du type Lachmann-Quentin," *Grai și suflet*, 4 [1929–30], 97–107). The Latinist Félix Peeters approved Bédier's approach for complicated traditions, finding Dom Quentin's method too rigid ("Les différents systèmes de classement des manuscrits," *Revue de l'Université de Bruxelles*, 36 [1930–31], 466–85). Although Mario Roques issued few theoretical pronouncements, he practiced Bédier's dictum of following a basic manuscript with few corrections in his editions of the *Roman de Renart* and of Chrétien's *Yvain*, *Lancelot*, and *Erec et Enide*; numerous other editors have done likewise. Eugène Vinaver refined the definition of errors requiring correction by cataloguing the kinds of error which result from the mechanical process of transcription; like Bédier, he advised editors "to aim, not at restoring the original work in every particular, but merely at lessening the damage done by copyists" ("Principles of Textual Emendation," in *Studies . . . Presented to Mildred K. Pope* [Manchester, Eng., 1939], pp. 351–69).[24] Bédier himself reaffirmed his position with a series of articles on the *Chanson de Roland* in 1937 and 1938 (see our note 3).

Most thoughtful editors soon acknowledged the shortcomings of Bédier's conservatism as an inflexible system. For example, the principle of adhering to a single basic manuscript constitutes an open invitation to laziness for any editor who wishes to avoid studying the manuscript tradition thoroughly. Giving unqualified precedence to the scribe means, in some cases, that the author will be slighted, for even the best and oldest copy must be imperfect. Theoretically, it is not clear whether Bédier was justified in basing what amounted to a new method on two specific cases—the *Roland* and the *Lai de l'Ombre*—which do in fact seem to merit the best-manuscript treatment.[25]

---

[24] Vinaver's article is reprinted in *Medieval Manuscripts and Textual Criticism*, ed. Kleinhenz, pp. 139–59.

[25] See, for example, Whitehead, "The Textual Criticism of the *Chanson de Roland*." Though these criticisms are raised by Romance scholars, they receive greater stress from classicists defending the traditional Lachmann position. See A. Dain, *Les Manuscrits* (Paris, 1949), pp. 155ff.; J. Andrieu, "Principes et recherches en critique textuelle," in *Mémorial des études latines . . . offert . . . à . . . J. Marouzeau* (Paris, 1943), pp. 458–74; Ludwig Bieler, *The Grammarian's Craft: An Introduction to Textual Criticism* (N.Y., 1965, rpt. from

Reaction to Dom Quentin's method by editors and theorists has generally been less favorable. Collomp thought it might prove useful for contaminated traditions (72–81), but Giorgio Pasquali considered it primitive, too mechanical and rigid for handling a complex tradition like that of the Vulgate (*Storia della tradizione e critica del testo* [Florence, 1934], pp. 178f.). William P. Shepard tried using the computational methods of Dom Quentin and of W. W. Greg (*Calculus of Variants* [Oxford, 1927]), in addition to the traditional Lachmann method, on several Old French and Old Provençal texts. The results he obtained differed so radically depending on the procedure used that none of the stemmas seemed reliable ("Recent Theories of Textual Criticism," *Modern Philology*, 28 [1930], 129–41). Emmanuel Walberg found the Benedictine's arguments circular themselves ("Prinzipien und Methoden für die Herausgabe alter Texte nach verschiedenen Handschriften," *Zeitschrift für romanische Philologie*, 51 [1931], 665–78). Legge, Coculesco, and Peeters also rejected Dom Quentin's method. After trying it, the Hellenist Alphonse Dain concluded that it offered nothing new beyond a numerical procedure for comparing variants and that traditional methods were more efficient (*Les Manuscrits* [Paris, 1949], pp. 162–64). To our knowledge, this method has not been used in preparing an edition of any Old French work; nevertheless, it has contributed to a redefinition of the concept of common error, which now encompasses both errors and innovations. Moreover, recently Robert Marichal defended the system, arguing that such reliance on numerical tabulations would lend itself to computer use, and in fact Dom J. Froger has based a method for classification by computer on distinctions made by Dom Quentin, substituting procedures drawn from set theory for the compar-

Classical Folia, 10 [1958], 3–42), pp. 18ff. The same objections are voiced by the Italian school of new philologists, e.g., Michele Barbi, in *La nuova filologia e l'edizione dei scrittori da Dante al Manzoni* (Florence, 1938; rpt. 1973), pp. xv–xxiv. See also Franca Brambilla Ageno's Appendice III, "I Metodi del Quentin e del Bédier," in *L'edizione critica dei testi volgari* (Medioevo e umanésimo, 22; Padua, 1975), pp. 153–62. All these scholars likewise reject Dom Quentin's method.

ison by threes.[26] So far, however, the value of the machine in textual criticism has not been established.

In defense of the traditional Lachmann system, a number of scholars have attempted to prove by common sense or the mathematics of probability that Bédier's "loi surprenante" (the predominance of the two-branch stemma) was the predictable result of manuscript transmission rather than a defect in the method of common error.[27] Their demonstrations have been reviewed by Timpanaro, in Appendix C to his historical study of the Lachmann method (112–35). The probabilistic arguments advanced by Maas, Fourquet, and Whitehead-Pickford have failed to gain wide approval because each proof started from assumptions about the typical stemma or the typical production of manuscripts which other scholars have considered unsound. In addition, it appears that many editors accustomed to dealing with the individual peculiarities of a single manuscript tradition have resisted such attempts to reduce the various problems created by scribes to mathematical formulas valid for the general case. Similarly, Castellani's theories about how the maximum number of copies might be produced when that was desirable encountered opposition because little is known about manuscript production in the high Middle Ages—not enough to construct a model—and in any case, the

---

[26] See Marichal, "La Critique des textes," in *L'Histoire et ses methodes*, ed. C. Samaran (Encyclopédie de la Pléiade, XI; Paris, 1961), p. 1291; Dom Froger, *La Critique des textes et son automatisation* (Initiation aux nouveautés de la science, 7; Paris, 1968); and H. Love, "The Computer and Literary Editing: Achievements and Prospects," in *The Computer in Literary and Linguistic Research* (Cambridge, 1971), pp. 47–56. Note that Marichal's Préface to Dom Froger's book stresses the limitations of the system described therein.

[27] For example, Paul Maas, *Textkritik* (Leipzig, 1927), trans. Barbara Flower (Oxford, 1958), pp. 47f.; Jean Fourquet, "Le Paradoxe de Bédier," in *Mélanges 1945*, II, *Etudes des lettres* (Pubns. de la Fac. des Lettres de l'Univ. de Strasbourg; Paris, 1946), pp. 1–16 (reviewed by Mario Roques in *Romania*, 1946–47, 116f.), and "Fautes communes ou innovations communes?", *Romania*, 70 (1948–49), 85–95; F. Whitehead and Cedric E. Pickford, "The Two-Branch Stemma," *BBSIA*, 3 (1951), 83–90; Jean Irigoin, "Stemmas bifides et états de manuscrits," *Revue de philologie*, 3ᵉ série, 28 (1954), 211–17; Arrigo Castellani, *Bédier avait-il raison? La Méthode de Lachmann dans les éditions de textes du moyen âge* (Fribourg, 1957). For down-to-earth assessments of Fourquet and Whitehead-Pickford, see E. B. Ham, "Textual Criticism and Common Sense," *RPh*, 12 (1958–59), 206–09; on Castellani, see Ham's review, *RPh*, 13 (1959–60), 190f. See also Marichal, pp. 1283–85.

likelihood of maximum reproduction of a given text is impossible to determine, as Castellani himself admitted.

Castellani reexamined the stemmatic data from which Bédier must have postulated his surprising law (Bédier gave few references) and concluded that, in stemmas constructed for Old French editions between 1872 and 1928, two-branch stemmas outnumber those with multiple branches in a ratio of four to one. Thus, even if the proportion is not quite so high as Bédier had claimed (105 two-branch stemmas out of 110 in 1928), it is still high enough to require explanation. This ratio is due in part, many scholars now agree, to the nature of manuscript transmission, although the attempt to explain this relationship mathematically has not succeeded. Bédier's charge that the Lachmann method fostered two-branch stemmas has been backed by Castellani and Timpanaro, in at least cases such as the following. First, a faulty archetype α gives rise to four independent copies, $a\ b\ c\ d$; a corrects α's faults on his own, while the three others merely reproduce them. These four copies, however, would probably be classified into two families, a and x (= bcd) if the editor failed to consider the possibility that a alone had corrected their common model. Second, because of contamination, two originally independent families present a number of common errors and may be classified as a single family.

For such cases, the stemma constructed by the common error method is shown, once again, to be simply a hypothesis, not the scientific truth which Gaston Paris had sought. In the face of this shortcoming, some of the mathematically inclined supporters of the method (e.g., Irigoin, Whitehead, and Pickford) called for more exhaustive study of manuscript transcriptions so that the hypothesis might be as sound as possible. Others, including Fourquet and Castellani, ended by endorsing a Bédierist reliance on a single basic manuscript for every case when a stemma is dubious or impossible.

As a result of Bédier's criticism, then, and of the controversy it provoked, the Lachmann method for manuscript classification and reconstitution of the archetype no longer commanded the almost automatic adherence of Old French editors after 1928. Some still continued trying to approximate the au-

thor's composition, although most of these now eschewed the
language reconstructions which had been customary since
1872. However, a great many Old French textual critics, from
conviction or prudence, took the safer course of reproducing
the redaction of a single manuscript with few corrections,[28]
despite criticism that favoring the scribe harms the author.[29]
As time went by, a few editors sought to dispel the uncertainty
hovering over Old French textual criticism by advocating tolerance for a variety of editing practices.

V. TOWARDS A NEW CONSENSUS?

In the years following Bédier's revolt against the common
error method, editors of Old French works which had been
preserved in several manuscripts agonized over how to establish the texts for their editions. Such a crisis of conscience was
most severe for those who were reluctant to adopt Bédier's
best-manuscript conservatism as the new universal formula.
Edward B. Ham summed up the dilemma and its practical consequences thus:

> Loosely stated, and in its most familiar terms, the usual
> problem which has harassed so many editors is, of
> course, that of the composite text versus reproduction of
> a so-called best manuscript. Should the editor in his crit-
> ical text incorporate all the emendations which, in his
> opinion, would contribute to a restoration of the origi-

---

[28] By 1933, Robert Bossuat—grudgingly—considered this practice standard among "les éditeurs modernes." See his reviews of *La Vie de saint Alexis*,
ed. J.-M. Meunier (Paris, 1933), and of Jean d'Arras, *Melusine*, ed. Louis Stouff
(Dijon, 1932), in *BEC*, 94 (1933), 376–79.

[29] See criticism of Roques's *Lancelot* edition by E. Vinaver in the *Mélanges
... Jean Fourquet* (Munich & Paris, 1969; rpt. in Eng., trans. Douglas Kelly, in
Medieval Manuscripts and Textual Criticism, pp. 160–66), pp. 355–61; also
the comments by Alfred Foulet in the *Jean Misrahi Memorial Volume* (Colum-
bia, S.C., 1977), 175–80, by David J. Shirt in *Studies ... Frederick Whitehead*
(Manchester, Eng., 1973), pp. 279–301, and by T. B. W. Reid, in "Chrétien de
Troyes and the Scribe Guiot," *Medium Ævum*, 45 (1976), 1–19.

nal? Or, instead, should the editor publish a good manuscript and thereby spare his medieval author the doubt-
ful benefits of the creative archaeology implicit in a
twentieth-century collaboration? If the first method is
followed, how does the editor avoid an outright patch-
work of readings from several manuscripts, a mosaic
which may easily fail to be either authentic or even con-
sistently medieval? If the second method is followed,
how does the editor fulfill his duty of shedding maximum light on his author's original work?[30]

Linked to this problem—sometimes, indeed, indistin-
guishable from it—was, and is, the dilemma of editorial subjectivity. How far should the editor go in emending his basic
text? How sure can he be that what he perceives as an error
would have been rejected by the author, or that the author
would have tolerated his emendation? This uncertainty affects
not only editors working with several manuscripts, but also
those dealing with a unique manuscript; and it intrudes its
troublesome presence whether the editor adopts a conservative
or reconstructive approach towards establishing the basic text.
Scholars may agree on some kinds of "obvious errors" which
even Bédier approved of correcting; other errors fall into what
Ham called the "twilight zones of emendation" (3).

Once faith in universal editorial formulas had been shak-
en, a pragmatic way to handle these problems was to posit a
methodological eclecticism allowing each editor to choose the
approach which suited his text's peculiar characteristics. As
we have seen, some editors availed themselves of this freedom
even in the heyday of the Lachmann method, but their practice
was hardly considered exemplary. A statement of principle
came as early as 1937 from the Princeton University team of
editors, headed by Edward C. Armstrong, who worked on the
Roman d'Alexandre. This well-liked romance survives in a
number of Old French redactions, presenting a complex manuscript tradition. Prior to Alexandre de Paris's reworking (ca.
1190), it circulated in a version now preserved in two divergent
and contaminated redactions, the Arsenal and Venice versions.

---

[30] *Textual Criticism and Jehan le Venelais* (Ann Arbor, 1946), p. 4.

Because it was impossible to reconstitute this early *Roman d'Alexandre* from its unfaithful descendants, the Armstrong group chose to publish the texts of these two manuscripts separately in critical editions which seldom depart from the manuscript text.[31] On the other hand, judging that there was sufficient evidence to reconstruct Alexandre de Paris's *Alexandre* from its score of surviving manuscripts plus fragments, the team attempted that feat in its second volume, defending this endangered procedure in terms which encouraged other editors to take advantage of the possibilities offered by individual manuscript traditions:

> There can be no inflexible rules for text editing, for each text constitutes a new problem and the right procedure is the one which best fits the individual situation. . . . An editor is faced with the necessity of choosing: he may publish one of these uncritical medieval editions, selecting the one which this twentieth-century editor deems best, or he may attempt, by a critical study of all medieval versions, to present a text nearer than any one of them to the antecedent work. Before the choice is made, it is essential that he ascertain, by a minute study of the manuscripts, how much evidence they offer regarding the prototype or prototypes, and that he weigh with equal attention the possible limitations upon the validity of that evidence. In some cases it may be indicated that he adhere closely to one manuscript, which gives a text which at least one man of the times found to his taste; in other instances the data may justify emendation.[32]

This pragmatic eclecticism was adopted and refined by Ham, a former member of the Armstrong team, in the Introduction to his second edition of the *Venjance Alixandre*, entitled *Textual Criticism and Jehan le Venelais*. Ham had pub-

---

[31] *The Medieval French 'Roman d'Alexandre,'* vol. I, *Text of the Arsenal and Venice Versions*, ed. Milan S. La Du (EM, 36; Princeton, 1937).

[32] *The Medieval French 'Roman d'Alexandre,'* vol. II, *Version of Alexandre de Paris, Text*, ed. Edward C. Armstrong, D. L. Buffum, Bateman Edwards, and L. F. H. Lowe (EM, 37; Princeton, 1937), pp. xviii–xix.

lished a first edition, based on manuscript *M* (Paris, B.N. fr. 24365) in 1931;[33] but subsequent analyses by the Armstrong group discredited *M* as the work of an intelligent and improvement-minded redactor-copyist, whose text is far removed from his model's, whereas *X* (British Library, Royal 19 D i), a late and clumsy redaction, now appeared closer to the twelfth-century original. Since it seemed impossible to justify a preference for either *X* or *M* as the only authoritative version of the poem and equally impossible to use the two manuscripts to reconstruct the archetype, Ham published a second edition based on *X*, in a kind of "afterthought scholarship" that he compared with Bédier's second edition of the *Lai de l'Ombre*. His Introduction had a double purpose: defending his new edition and exploring the illustrative value of such a procedure for editorial techniques in Old French.

Like the Armstrong team, Ham foresaw no possibility of a return to universal editing formulas: "The day for iron-clad delimiting definitions, generalized for all texts, is past and should never have existed" (9). As replacement for the rigid old norms, he advocated the Armstrong principle of letting the textual tradition determine the editing procedure to be employed. Ham qualified this with two basic axioms to govern all editions: "First, an editor must provide a table of variant readings sufficiently extensive to permit the fullest possible control of the manuscripts." For longer texts, "intelligent application of the axiom concerning variants requires carefully chosen criteria for inclusion and exclusion. Such criteria can be determined only by conditions inherent in the manuscript tradition of each separate text" (6f.). "The second general axiom requires a search for the fullest possible light on the readings of the lost original. The individual problem in this connection involves, obviously, the precise extent to which reconstituted readings shall appear in a given edited text" (7).

In addition to these axiomatic responsibilities to the scribe and to the author, Ham formulated a corollary concerning the editor's obligation to take the reader into his confidence: "No medieval text which raises genuine difficulties should be pub-

---

[33] *Jehan le Nevelon—la Venjance Alixandre* (EM, 27; Princeton, 1931).

lished without at least a brief excursus enabling the reader to judge the personal attitudes of the editor" (3). Subjective decisions are unavoidable in editing, but if the editor attempts to justify his decisions, for instance, on accepting some readings of the basic manuscript while rejecting others, he will provide the reader with the information to make up his own mind.

Ham's endorsement of methodological eclecticism, tempered with the axioms above, followed—and was no doubt influenced by—analogous developments in the Italian school of new philologists. During the 1930s, in the wake of the attacks by Bédier and Dom Quentin, some Italian scholars began to reevaluate the traditional Lachmann method in an effort to rehabilitate what was workable and modify what was not. Pasquali's authoritative volume, *Storia della tradizione e critica del testo*, grew specifically out of a long review of Maas's *Textkritik* (Leipzig, 1927), a manual adamantly defending the Lachmann method which Pasquali considered too abstract.[34] In reaction, he examined the real problems posed by the manuscript traditions of certain Greek, Latin, and Italian works, suggesting ingenious solutions for each case and drawing from them general principles. Barbi, in *La nuova filologia e l'edizione dei nostri scrittori da Dante al Manzoni*, proposed similar principles, illustrated in examples from well-known Italian texts. Pasquali, in particular, demonstrated that many of the Lachmann rules were too rigid and that for any manuscript tradition which was not purely mechanical, where the scribe had thought he understood what he was copying, no universal editorial recipe could be valid. He affirmed the importance of the editor's judgment in every stage of the editing process, from collation of manuscripts to selection of variants—not merely arbitrary judgment, but an informed judgment versed in the author's milieu and style and in every aspect of the manuscript tradition. Above all, he stressed that each text is different and requires a different editorial approach. However, both Pasquali and Barbi believed the editor's

---

[34] Pasquali's review appeared in *Gnomon*, 5 (1929), 417–35, 498–521. For discussion of the revised editions of Maas's handbook and its reception in Italy and France, see Luciano Canfora, "Critica textualis in caelum revocata," *Belfagor*, 23 (1968), 361–64.

fundamental duty to be the reconstitution of the author's original from the entire manuscript tradition; in other words, the
methodological innovations they prescribed comprised only
modifications and genuine refinements of the Lachmann method. To their way of thinking, the author's text must always
come first; the only "best manuscript" would be the author's
holograph, so they naturally denounced any Bédieristic con-
servation of a later scribal redaction as the resort of scholars
unwilling or unable to discover the authentic text. "La verità
non concede se stessa agli stupidi," averred Pasquali (125).
Hence, a critical text established at the risk of conjectural
emendations is preferable to an edition based on one manuscript or tradition, provided that the editor justify his decisions
to the reader.

The new philologists' optimism about recovering the author's text has not won over many Old French editors in the
skeptical northern climes of France, Great Britain, and the
United States, but it has exerted enormous influence in Italy.[35]
Nevertheless, under pressure from linguists and language historians who need genuine manuscript texts for study, the Italian philologists have modified their position on language reconstruction and now recommend adopting the forms and
orthography of a single basic manuscript in a dialect resem-
bling that of the author.[36] This is, of course, the position taken
by almost all Old French editors since Bédier. Also, the new
philologists' emphasis on tailoring the editorial technique to

---

[35] See A. Roncaglia on "Critica testuale" in *Cultura neolatina*, 12 (1952),
281–83; see also Alberto Chiari's presentation for graduate students, "La edizione critica," in *Tecnica e teoria letteraria*, ed. M. Tubini, G. Getto, B. Migliorini, A. Chiari, and V. Pernicone (Problemi ed orientamenti critici di lingua
e di letteratura italiana; 2nd ed., Milan, 1951), pp. 231–95; and Alberto Vàrvaro's comparative evaluation of several methods, which hints at tolerance of
best-manuscript editions, "Critica dei testi classica e romanza: Problemi comuni ed esperienze diverse," *Rendiconti della Academia di Archeologia, Lettere e Belle Arti di Napoli*, 45 (1970), 73–117. Recently Franca Brambilla Ageno
published an excellent manual for editing Italian texts in the new philology
tradition: *L'edizione critica dei testi volgari* (see n. 25). For a review of the
manual, see Mary B. Speer, "In Defense of Philology: Two New Guides to
Textual Criticism," *RPh*, 32 (Feb. 1979).
[36] See Gianfranco Contini, "Rapporti fra la filologia (come critica testuale)
e la linguistica romanza," in *Actes du XIIᵉ Congrès International de Linguistique et Philologie Romanes, 1968* (Bucharest, 1970), I, 47–65; and Brambilla
Ageno, pp. 121–28.

fit the text has produced one significant exception to their neo-Lachmannism: Domenico de Robertis advocates separate best-manuscript editions of each version for the anonymous thirteenth-century narrative *cantari*; his reasons for rejecting the combinatory Lachmann method are reminiscent of Bédier's and could possibly lead to a methodological détente with more pragmatic editing philosophies.[37]

Meanwhile, the plea for eclecticism launched by Armstrong and Ham has evoked little direct response, either here or abroad.[38] Was it perhaps considered so obvious that everyone except the new philologists has taken it for granted and accorded it tacit approval as the established consensus? This seems unlikely because in an independent article published in 1955, István Frank urged editors to choose the "combinatory" (Lachmannian) or "selective" (best-manuscript) method according to the demands of their individual manuscript traditions, as though the idea were new. For many lyric *chansons*, which probably had multiple originals and which come down to us in *chansonniers* that are often the result of skillful compilation and borrowing on the part of a scribal editor, Frank believed that the combinatory method was less satisfactory than the selective one ("De l'art d'éditer les textes lyriques," in *Recueil de travaux offert à M. Clovis Brunel* [Paris, 1955], I, 463–75). Frank's emphasis on the need for studying the manuscript tradition thoroughly and justifying any editorial intervention is echoed in Marichal's introduction to textual criticism for historians and in Whitehead and Pickford's retrospective of Old French editing since the 1913 edition of the

---

[37] "Problemi di metodo nell' edizione dei cantari," in *Studi e problemi di critica testuale*, ed. Raffaele Spongano (Bologna, 1961), pp. 119–38; cf. Brambilla Ageno's misgivings, pp. 234–40.

[38] In a review of Ham's book (*Speculum*, 22 [1947], 468–70), Urban T. Holmes, Jr., reaffirmed the Bédierist position, questioning even the need for metrical corrections: "Why was every scribe except the first a careless ignoramus, and every author a flawless wielder of Old French metrics and case endings?" Three years after the publication of Ham's essay, Charles A. Knudson called on "Old French scholars whose word carries authority . . . to formulate standards and to point out ways in which younger scholars may follow with confidence"; see "The Publication of Old French Texts: Some Comments and Suggestions," *Speculum*, 24 (1949), 510–15.

Lai de l'Ombre. Whitehead and Pickford welcome what they diagnose as the waning of extreme conservatism in favor of more traditional (i.e., Lachmannian) methods, but they emphasize that Bédier's skepticism has caused traditional editors to lower their expectations. Even with the most careful examination of the manuscript filiations, an editor can now aspire to no more than "a partial reconstitution of the original text."

Nevertheless, if textual critics in Old French have hesitated to back methodological eclecticism explicitly, they have been publishing editions which take advantage of the current tolerance for different methods. Contemporary editions of texts contained in three or more manuscripts bear witness, on the one hand, to the endurance of the traditional Lachmann method and the vitality of the Bédierist reaction and, on the other, to innovations developed to handle special textual problems, particularly in the matter of establishing the text. Nearly all editors grant the wisdom of trying to understand the relationships of the various manuscripts and of depicting those affiliations in a stemma, if possible; what use to make of the stemma remains the heart of the editing problem. To give an idea of the variety of approaches now practiced, we shall describe briefly a few editions published since 1950.

Reconstituting the archetype. For an edition of Henri d'Andeli's *Lai d'Aristote* (Bibl. de la Fac. de Philos. et Lettres de l'Univ. de Liège, CXXIII; Paris, 1951), Maurice Delbouille classified the five manuscripts of the *Lai* into two families: *ABC*, with *AB* and *C* as subgroups; *DE*, with great differences between *D* and *E*. He concluded that the *ABC* family represents a shortened form of the text; *DE*, a fuller, more authentic version. Despite its lacunas and awkward passages, *D* offers the fewest omissions and additions. *E* is marred by lacunas, scribal interpolations, physical gaps, and Picard spelling which was not the author's. Therefore, Delbouille took *D* as his basic manuscript and adopted its forms; he corrected *D*'s text from *E* whenever *ABCE* agreed against *D* and whenever *D* was faulty: some 168 times in 579 lines. This is a limited reconstitution which respects one manuscript's orthography but gives the author's creation (that is, the editor's conception of it) precedence over any single scribal redaction.

Jean Rychner allowed himself to intervene even more in his editions of Marie de France's *Lais*. For *Lanval* (TLF; Geneva, 1958), he published diplomatic transcriptions of the four manuscripts and a critical text based on *H*, an Anglo-Norman manuscript (British Library, Harley 978), modifying *H* in certain situations when the other manuscripts opposed it (see pp. 15f. of his Introduction). Adopting the linguistic forms imposed on the *Lais* by Karl Warnke in his 1885 edition, Rychner changed the morphology and orthography of *H* to conform to what he thought represented Marie's own language. To handle all the *Lais* (CFMA; Paris, 1973), Rychner opted for a more conservative edition, again based on *H*, but now aiming only to correct *H*'s errors. Nevertheless, he regularized *H*'s Anglo-Norman orthography, morphology, and meter for the sake of clarity and uniformity. Not entirely satisfied with this compromise between the hypercorrection of Warnke's reconstituted archetype and Alfred Ewert's nearly absolute fidelity to *H* (Oxford, 1944), Rychner yearned for the far-reaching interventions permitted to past editors: "Son défaut [i.e., of his textual "cuisine"] est de marier une morphologie correcte, en elle-même parfaitement justifiée, à la graphie caractéristique d'une langue qui ignorait justement la correction morphologique. Comment ne pas évoquer alors avec nostalgie la solution choisie par E. Hoepffner [Strasbourg, 1921], qui imprimait le texte de *H* dans la graphie continentale de *S*?" (xxviii).

Basic manuscript plus controllers. The control method was devised by Alexandre Micha for handling the contaminated manuscript tradition of Chrétien de Troyes's romances: *Prolégomènes à une édition de 'Cligès'* (Annales de l'Univ. de Lyon, 3ᵉ série, fasc. 8; Paris, 1938) and *La Tradition manuscrite des romans de Chrétien de Troyes* (Paris, 1939). When an editor is unable to establish a stemma but succeeds in dividing the manuscripts into different groups, he may select the best representative of the least innovative group as his basic manuscript and use the best manuscripts of the other groups as controllers. If these manuscripts disagree, he will follow his basic manuscript when its isolated reading is superior to that of the control manuscripts and abandon the base when its individual reading is clearly a scribal reworking. Nevertheless, Micha's

edition of *Cligés* (CFMA; Paris, 1965) is characterized by extreme respect for his basic manuscript.[39] Albert Henry has used
the control method successfully in his editions of romances by
Adenet le Roi.[40]

Synoptic edition. In an edition of the *Chanson de Roland*
(Milan, 1971), Cesare Segre presented the texts of both *Roland*
families concurrently. He adopted, with modifications, the
two-branch stemma proposed by Theodor Müller and endorsed
by Bédier: *O* alone here represents the α family, while all the
other Old French texts (*V⁴CV⁷PLT*) and foreign translations derive from the β ancestor. Segre's edition is designed to permit
comparison of the two families. He printed the text of *O*, corrected for scribal errors, in roman type; in italics and with
special numbering, he inserted the text of V^4, the oldest French
representative of the β family, for passages where the β tradition contains material not found in *O*. Segre agrees with Bédier
that most of these additions constitute β *remaniements* and
should not be attributed to the archetype of both α and β families (as was the case in Stengel's edition). In the variant apparatus, Segre examined the readings derived from β which
may shed some light on *O*, and he evaluated the authenticity
of each reading; however, anywhere that at least one β representative concurs with *O*, he assumed that such a passage occurred in their common archetype and gave no other variants
for it. Thus, the apparatus does not perform its usual function
of justifying the edited text; instead, it serves to document the
stratigraphic reading of different stages in the manuscript tradition of the epic.

Divergent texts on facing pages. When a text appears in
several manuscripts which offer two or more very different

---

[39] Perhaps in part because Mario Roques had set the pattern of faithfully
adhering to the Guiot copy (Paris, B.N. fr. 794) in the CFMA editions of Chrétien's romances. See Roques's rather critical review of Micha's dissertations in
Romania, 68 (1944–45), 211–19.

[40] Vols. 1–3, *Biographie et introduction, Buevon de Conmarchis, Les En-
fances Ogier* (Rijksuniversitet te Gent, Werken uitgegeven door de faculteit van
de wijsbegeerte en letteren, 106, 115, 121; Bruges, 1951–56); vol. 4, *Berte aus
grans piés* (Paris, 1963); vol. 5, *Cleomadés* (Univ. de Bruxelles, Travaux de la
Fac. de Philos. et Lettres, XLVI; Brussels, 1971). See Alfred Foulet's review of
Cleomadés, *RPh*, 30 (1976–77), 284–86.

versions of the work, some editors have decided to place them on facing pages. Having determined that one could not choose between the Short and Long Redactions of the *Continuations* of Chrétien's *Perceval*, William Roach put editions of both on opposing pages (vols. III–IV; Philadelphia, 1952–71). To illustrate his observations about scribal redactors' propensity for transforming *fabliaux* through variants, reworking, and corruptions, Rychner juxtaposed most of the different versions of seventeen *fabliaux* in *Contributions à l'étude des fabliaux* (Neuchâtel, 1960), volume II, *Textes*.

Best-manuscript editions. Adherence to a single basic manuscript remains the method of choice for many editors. The extent to which the editor intervenes varies according to the text, the editor, and the series publishing the edition. For instance, Guy Raynaud de Lage rarely modified the text of his basic manuscript for the *Roman de Thèbes* (2 vols.; CFMA; Paris, 1966–68) and published no variants from other manuscripts, while Joseph Palermo published variants from manuscript *B* to shed light on his closely followed basic manuscript *V* of the *Roman de Cassidorus* (2 vols.; SATF; Paris, 1963–64).

In passing, it is curious to observe that the more adventurous and judgmental methods for handling texts in the post-Bédier period have often been practiced by scholars from outside the hexagon of France. Perhaps the French love of system and clarity favors the best-manuscript edition as the only logically consistent method left to us.

The vicissitudes of the last 150 years amply illustrate Bédier's maxim about theoretical flux in editing and the influence of styles and powerful personalities in this area of Old French scholarship. Two general lessons which can be drawn from this historical overview should be kept in mind by editors and readers of all medieval French texts:

(1) A purely mechanical system of editing (even if such a thing exists) is inappropriate for Old French texts; hence, the editor's informed judgment or subjectivity must play a crucial role in each stage of the editing process. Any edition is a conjecture; it also constitutes a critical interpretation of the text.

(2) In establishing the text, the editor has to reckon with three basic factors: the author, the scribe, and the reader. Circumstances of the manuscript tradition often help determine whether priority is given to the author's text or the scribe's copy, but the editor must be aware how fundamental this decision is. And he must inform the reader as fully as possible about his attitudes and justify any debatable decisions he may make.

In other words, editing is not a science, but an art.[41]

---

[41] Edmond Faral reached this conclusion some years ago: "L'édition des textes est un art qui, comme tous les arts, demande de l'à-propos, le sentiment de convenances diverses et, avant tout, la faculté de discerner entre le possible, le probable et le certain"; see "A propos de l'édition des textes anciens: le cas du manuscrit unique," in *Recueil de travaux offert à M. Clovis Brunel* (Paris, 1955), I, 411.

2

Preparing the Text

I. SCRIBES AND EDITORS

1. The Old French Text

A literary text "published" in our 1150–1300 period was handwritten on vellum (rarely on paper). Each gathering or quire (French *cahier*) was normally composed of four sheets of vellum folded to make eight leaves (folios), with writing on the front (recto) and back (verso) of each leaf, for a total of sixteen pages. The leaves of each gathering were sewn together firmly, and after the scribe(s) had filled a number of quires with a work or collection of works, the gatherings were bound to form a book. Such a handwritten volume is called a codex.

Since we seldom, in fact almost never, possess the author's holograph for our period, each manuscript which confronts us is a faulty copy, at some remove from the author's original composition. For instance, although Chrétien de Troyes composed his romances between about 1160 and about 1190, no extant manuscript of them antedates the first decades of the thirteenth century.

The scribe's aim was ordinarily to produce a fair copy, but where he understood the text he was transcribing—as scribes usually did for Old French texts—a "fair copy" had no resemblance to the photographic copies we know today; it might range from a generally faithful reproduction of a model to an extensive revision which amounted to a new version of the work in question. Thus, in most cases, the scribe must be considered the editor of the text he copied, and the modern editor's edition is really a re-edition.

2. The Legibility and Intelligibility of Manuscripts

Extant literary manuscripts are usually written in a neat and pleasing hand; yet their legibility does not make them immediately intelligible. The modern reader intent on grasping the text's meaning may be hindered by any one of several obstacles: the lack of standard spelling, the occasional running together of words, the absence of diacritical marks and modern punctuation, and the use of abbreviations.

3. Types of Editions

After choosing the text he wishes to edit, the prospective editor must determine which of the three types of edition is appropriate for his text and his audience: a facsimile, diplomatic, or critical edition. Nowadays an editor will almost always be preparing a critical edition, but he should be aware of the availability and usefulness of the other types.

4. Facsimile Editions

The most faithful reproduction of an Old French text is obtained through photography. This type of edition is best suited to a masterpiece preserved in a single manuscript (e.g., the Oxford *Roland*) and to valuable manuscripts containing collections of poems or lyrics with musical notation. The libraries which own such manuscripts now often restrict access to them in order to protect them from wear and tear, so only by photographic reproduction can they be available to a large number of scholars. For the reader's benefit, a detailed paleographical analysis should accompany any edition of this type.

Examples of facsimile reproductions:

Cest Daucasī & de Nicolete, reproduced in Photo-facsimile and Type-transliteration from the unique Ms. in the Bibliothèque Nationale at Paris, Fonds français 2168, by the care of F. W. Bourdillon. Oxford, 1896.

La Chanson de Roland, reproduction phototypique du manuscrit Digby 23 de la Bodleian Library d'Oxford. Introduction du comte Alexandre de Laborde et étude paléographique de M. Ch. Samaran. SATF. Paris, 1933.

Les Chansonniers des troubadours et des trouvères, publiés en facsimilé et transcrits en notation moderne par Jean Beck et Madame Louise Beck. Corpus Cantilenarum Medii Aevi. Numéro 1: *Le Chansonnier Cangé* (Paris, B.N. fr. 846). 2 vols. Numéro 2: *Le Manuscrit du Roi* (Paris, B.N. fr. 844). 2 vols. Philadelphia, 1927–38.

Chrestien de Troyes: Le Manuscrit d'Annonay, ed. Albert Pauphilet. Paris, 1934. (Fragments of *Cligés, Yvain*, and *Perceval*.)

Fabliaux, dits et contes en vers du XIIIe siècle; fac-similé du manuscrit français 837 de la Bibliothèque Nationale, ed. Henri Omont. Paris, 1932.

MS. Bibliothèque Nationale anc. fonds fr. 1450, reproduced by the MLA in photo facsimile. MLA Collection of Photographic Facsimiles, no. 143. New York, 1930. (*Troie, Eneas*, first part of *Brut, Erec et Enide, Perceval, Cligés, Yvain, Lancelot*, remaining part of *Brut, Dolopathos*.)

Le Manuscrit 19152 du fonds français de la Bibliothèque Nationale, reproduction phototypique, ed. Edmond Faral. Paris, 1934. (*Fabliaux, contes, Partonopeus de Blois, Floire et Blancheflor*, etc.)

5. Diplomatic Editions

Strictly speaking, a diplomatic edition is a printed representation of all the particulars of a manuscript text, without benefit of such adjustments as the separation of words run together and the addition of diacritical marks and modern punctuation. Even the abbreviations, reproduced in type as accurately as possible, remain unexpanded. The term *diplomatic edition* comes from diplomatics, the branch of paleography that deals with legal and official documents, diplomas, and charters.

For Old French, diplomatic editions are useful in manuals of paleography, where plates illustrating specimens of medieval script are followed by their transcription; here the abbreviations may be expanded, with the added letters in italics. A second use of diplomatic editions is also primarily pedagogic: they serve to display just what the manuscript text contains, before any editorial intervention, but in a printed form which can be read more easily and rapidly than the manuscript or its photographic reproduction. In addition, reviewers of critical editions often turn to diplomatic editions (and facsimiles) to verify an editor's transcription of his basic manuscript or his handling of variant readings.

The usefulness of diplomatic editions in teaching and textual criticism, combined with renewed interest in the transformations undergone by a single text in its medieval history, has prompted the development of a modified form which is sometimes called an interpretative diplomatic edition. Here the work of the editor has already begun: the words are separated, the abbreviations are resolved in italics, and occasionally modern punctuation has even been added.

Examples of strictly diplomatic editions:

Foerster, W., and E. Koschwitz, eds. *Altfranzösisches Übungsbuch*. 4th ed. Leipzig, 1911. (Reichenauer and Kassel Glossaries, Strasbourg Oaths, *Sainte Eulalie, Vie de saint Alexis*, etc.)

Stengel, Edmund, ed. *Das altfranzösische Rolandslied*. Genauer Abdruck der Oxforder Hs. Digby 23. Heilbronn, 1878.

Examples of interpretative diplomatic editions:

Mortier, Raoul, ed. *Les Textes de la Chanson de Roland*. 10 vols. Paris, 1940–44. (Diplomatic editions of *O, V⁴, C, P, L,* and *T*; facsimiles of *V⁴* and *V⁷*.)

Rychner, Jean, ed. Eustache d'Amiens, *Du Bouchier d'Abevile*. Texte critique et édition diplomatique des cinq manuscrits. TLF. Geneva, 1975.

6. Critical Editions

A critical edition calls for the active intervention of the editor. One part of his work is making the manuscript text accessible to the modern reader by expanding abbreviations, separating words, inserting diacritical marks, and adding modern punctuation. But he must interfere still further to correct the scribe's errors, and he should provide the reader with the materials necessary to interpret the text and control the editor's treatment of it. These supportive materials include the introduction, variants, notes, glossary, and table of proper names. The making of a scholarly critical edition is the subject of our discussion from now on. The rest of Part 2 deals with preparing the text itself; Part 3, with the interpretative framework which will support the critically edited text.

II. GATHERING THE MATERIALS

1. Direct Testimony

Once the editor has selected the text for his edition, he determines the identity and location of all manuscripts and fragments containing that work—the direct witnesses. Standard bibliographies of Old French literature provide a useful starting place for this research: e.g., Robert Bossuat, *Manuel bibliographique de la littérature française du moyen âge* (Melun, 1951), and two *Suppléments* (Paris, 1955–61); D. C. Cabeen, gen. ed., and U. T. Holmes, Jr., ed., *A Critical Bibliography of French Literature*; I, *The Mediaeval Period* (Syracuse, 1947; rev. ed., 1952); Gustav Gröber, *Grundriss der romanischen Philologie*, vol. II (Strasbourg, 1902); Gaston Raynaud, *Bibliographie des chansonniers français des XIIIᵉ etXIVᵉ siècles*, 2 vols. (Paris, 1884); H. Spanke, G. *Raynauds Bibliographie des altfranzösisches Liedes, neu bearbeitet und ergänzt* (Leyde, 1955); Brian Woledge, *Bibliographie des romans et nouvelles en prose française antérieurs à 1500* (PRF; Geneva, 1954) and *Supplément* (1975); Woledge and H. P. Clive, *Répertoire des plus anciens textes en prose française depuis 842 jusqu'aux premières années du XIIIᵉ siècle* (PRF; Geneva, 1964). In addition, the Section Romane of the Institut de Recherche et d'Histoire des Textes (40, avenue d'Iéna, 75016 Paris) serves as a kind of clearing house for editors and editions.

The editor should then obtain a photographic reproduction of each manuscript, either microfilm or photocopy, unless there are good reasons for not doing so. As a start, check to see if any of the manuscripts needed appear in the list of reproductions (microfilms or rotographs) of many manuscripts and rare printed books procured by the MLA and now on deposit in the Library of Congress; the list appears in *PMLA*, 65 (1950), 289–332. Other microfilms can usually be obtained through the Section Romane (mentioned above) or through the libraries which own the manuscripts.

While he is gathering his materials, the editor should also be assembling a dossier of information about each manuscript: its contents, physical appearance, and descriptions of it which appear in manuscript catalogues, journals, and other editions.

The editor may also wish to consult the "Bibliography of Editions and Translations in Progress" which is published annually in the January issue of *Speculum* and editorial guidelines issued by the Center for Scholarly Editions at the MLA (see "The Center for Scholarly Editions: An Introductory Statement," *PMLA*, 92 [1977], 583–97).

2. Assigning Sigla

Each manuscript should be assigned a siglum: a letter or abbreviation for easy reference. Often the siglum is the first letter of the name of the city or library where the manuscript is now kept or of the collector who once owned it, though sometimes various other factors influence the choice of sigla. For example, the two manuscripts in verse of the *Roman des Sept Sages* are Paris, B.N. fr. 1553, known as *K* because H. A. Keller first edited it in 1836, and Chartres, Bibl. munic. 620 (destroyed in 1944), called *C* for its domicile. Capital letters are used for manuscripts containing the entire text or a major portion of it; lower-case letters, for fragments. Usually sigla are italicized.

When a work has been edited before, the new editor should retain the sigla adopted by his predecessors.

3. Indirect Testimony

In addition to copies of manuscripts, the editor should also collect materials which give him secondhand information about the text—the indirect witnesses. These include sources, analogues, imitations, translations, and quotations from or allusions to the work in later compositions. They may, or may not, be helpful in determining the author or place of composition, in classifying the manuscripts, or in establishing the text. For example, the *Roman d'Athis et Prophilias* serves as an indirect witness for the *Roman de Thèbes* because it contains a rather long summary of *Thèbes* (vv. 5769ff.). Likewise, *Athis et Prophilias* constitutes a source for the *Roman de Cristal et Clarie*, which incorporates substantial passages lifted from *Athis et Prophilias* into its text, while *Cristal et Clarie* is, in turn, an indirect witness for its source.

4. Transcribing a Manuscript

Let us begin with the simplest case: the single manuscript. For both accuracy and convenience, it is wise to transfer microfilm to photographic enlargements, rather than transcribe it directly through the use of a microfilm reader. At first the editor should probably transcribe the photocopy diplomatically, that is, without expanding abbreviations or separating agglomerated words. In this way he can study the scribe's system of abbreviating and dividing words before he makes a definitive transcription.

As he begins the initial transcription, the editor may find it helpful to draw up a chart showing how the scribe forms each letter and what abbreviations and punctuation signs he uses. He should make a note of any letters which seem especially confusing in the scribe's hand, such as u and n, or c and t.

5. Collating Manuscripts

When two or more manuscripts exist, they should be collated in order to choose the one which will serve as basic manuscript. The comparison will focus on the physical condition and completeness of the manuscripts, each one's age and dialect, and the general quality of the scribe's copy, as well as its probable relation to the author's original text. To be sure, the importance of any of these factors depends on the individual work, and inevitably an element of subjectivity is bound to condition the editor's choice unless he is dealing with a clear-cut case, such as the Oxford manuscript of the assonanced *Roland* or manuscript *A* of Joinville's *Vie de saint Louis*. In less obvious cases, the respective merits and demerits of every manuscript should be carefully and fairly weighed.

In most instances, a comparison of the texts in the various manuscripts is also part of establishing a stemma. This requires a preliminary transcription of some portion of all the manuscripts. If the choice of the basic manuscript is not obvious, the editor draws on his study of the manuscripts' qualities to select a likely candidate as tentative base, and he transcribes that manuscript in full. Then he notes the variant readings from all the other manuscripts. When the composition in question is quite long, the editor may decide to limit his collation to a number of well-chosen passages. If so, he should exercise care in choosing these passages and evaluate the results of his collation cautiously; a manuscript's affiliation with others may vary from place to place. (On constructing a stemma, see the following chapter.)

Once the basic manuscript has been chosen, it should be transcribed diplomatically in its entirety. This may be done either on the pages of a notebook or on loose sheets to be collected in a ring- or spring-binder. Index cards, though excellent for the notes, glossary, and table of proper names, are less convenient for transcriptions, especially for texts of any length, since they cannot easily be flipped back and forth whenever the editor wants to check a previous passage—just as a scholar working in a library finds it far easier to thumb through the pages of a catalogue than to delve into the packed drawers of a card index. Also, when the editor begins to link the variants to the text of the basic manuscript, he may find it handier to work with loose leaves, rather than a bound notebook, because he can interleave the variants between the pages of the text.

6. Collating against Previous Editions

If a previous editor chose the same basic manuscript, the present editor should compare his transcription with his predecessor's text. He might discover copying errors of his own.

7. Examining the Manuscripts Themselves

Whenever possible, the editor should examine the manuscripts in person, for peculiarities like binding and signature irregularities and changes in ink colors cannot be detected in microfilms or photocopies. Dust, tears in the parchment, or a slight fold in a page may cause uncertainty which can be resolved by consulting the original. Special attention should be paid to the small holes which may appear in the vellum. Sometimes, in the photocopies, the letters of the next folio (recto) or the preceding folio (verso) show through such a hole, and the editor working only from a photocopy may unwittingly transcribe letters which do not belong to a given passage.

III. CLASSIFYING THE MANUSCRIPTS
AND ESTABLISHING THE TEXT

1. Purpose of the Classification

If the text to be edited has been preserved in three or more manuscripts, the editor should attempt to classify these manuscripts and diagram their relationships by means of a stemma (genealogical tree). The purpose of the stemma is to depict, in graphic form, the affinities of the various manuscripts and their kinship with their lost common ancestor, the archetype.

The use to which the editor puts the stemma depends on two important factors: the nature of the manuscript tradition, which determines the reliability of the stemma and even the possibility of establishing one (see sections 4 and 10 below), and his own editorial philosophy. Traditionally an editor utilized his stemma to identify trustworthy manuscripts and to reconstruct the author's original text from the inevitably faulty copies which survived. Since the 1920s, editors who mistrust the procedures of stemma construction or deal with manuscripts which resist precise classification make more limited use of the stemma; they refer to it for selecting a single manuscript to serve as basic manuscript and for choosing control manuscripts to provide corrections when the base has erroneous readings. The stemma provides the editor with a valuable touchstone for assaying the merits and demerits of his basic manuscript, but he should always remember that a stemma is no more than a hypothesis.

2. Stemma Terminology

By convention, capital letters—usually in italics—denote manuscripts containing the entire text or a major part of it, while lower-case letters—also in italics usually—are reserved for fragments.

In stemmas letters also serve to designate the hypothetical intermediaries which separate the extant manuscripts from their common ancestor, the lost archetype, i.e., the author's holograph or some already faulty copy of it. While there is general agreement on using the symbols A (archetype) or O (original) for the imagined common ancestor of the surviving manuscripts, no such understanding obtains for the hypothetical intermediaries. Some editors use lower-case Greek letters (α, β, γ) to represent them; others prefer lower-case roman letters, usually not in italics (x, y, z). But all such designations remain matters of the editor's own choice. In the stemma reproduced in section 9 below, the symbols A, B, and C′ represent hypothetical intermediaries corresponding to x, y, z or α, β, γ in other stemmas.

In some stemmas solid lines joining manuscripts or families indicate primary relationships, while broken lines denote links of secondary importance—the results of *consultatio* or *contaminatio* (see section 3).

3. Evaluating the Scribes

The raw materials for constructing a stemma are derived from a thoughtful collation of the manuscripts with an eye to sorting them out into groups or families. In addition to noticing how each manuscript resembles or diverges from the others, the editor should evaluate the scribe's personal idiosyncrasies and his fidelity to his model. Bear in mind that exact fidelity to a model was never achieved, and seldom desired, by medieval scribes copying a vernacular work which they understood. It is, in fact, axiomatic that the dullest scribes produced the most faithful copies, for the brighter, more imaginative ones sought to improve on their models.

Several terms may be useful for characterizing the quality of transmission represented in a manuscript. With a straightforward transmission (*traditio*), the scribe copied one manuscript, more or less faithfully, depending on its condition and his abilities and temperament. However, even the most painstaking copy will be marred by errors of some sort, as every note-taker knows. Matters become more complicated when the scribe, instead of following just one manuscript, has a second manuscript at his disposal. He may then decide to borrow from it a few words (*consultatio*) or liberal doses of the text (*contaminatio*), or he may thoroughly blend together the versions of the two manuscripts (*conflatio*). His eclectic borrowing might even involve a third manuscript.

Whether the scribe has one model or several, he may make deliberate changes in the text (*innovatio*); these changes include correcting errors in his model(s), linguistic modernizing, and adapting the content to suit a new audience. A special kind of *innovatio* is the deliberate shortening of a text to produce an abbreviated redaction: "les scribes qui mangent le texte."

Occasionally a relatively late manuscript contains a reading which is superior to that offered by any other manuscript and which seems to hark back to the archetype. Such a reading may be due to a flash of intuition on the scribe's part (*divinatio*), a felicitous result of his attempt to improve on his model, or to his consultation of a manuscript no longer extant.

4. Characterizing the Manuscript Tradition

As he assesses each scribe's fidelity to his exemplar, the editor will be forming an opinion about the nature of the whole manuscript tradition. Was the text a kind of classic which inspired respect in all its copyists and suffered little deliberate rewriting? Or was it one which seemed to invite scribes to collaborate unrestrainedly with the author in improving and adapting the text for new readers? Each of these cases represents the end point of a continuum for describing the manuscript tradition, and most texts fall somewhere in the middle, tending towards one extreme or the other; it is important to remember that the difference between them is one of degree, not one of substance. Critics have called the end points of this continuum by various names, all of which contrast the fixed quality of some traditions with the inconstancy of others: thus, Dom Quentin opposed "dead texts" to "living" ones; Pasquali, closed recensions to open recensions; and Vàrvaro, quiescent traditions to active traditions.

For some texts, there may have been two or more authorial redactions, with the result that surviving manuscripts represent distinctly different archetypes.

5. The Basis of Stemma Construction: The Common Error

Traditionally the basis for determining manuscript groupings has been the concept of error: an aberration so peculiar that it seems virtually impossible for more than one scribe to have introduced it into the text. If two manuscripts share a significant number of common errors, they must be related: either (a) one is copied from the other, or (b) both descend from a common model. The difficulty here is that the definition of a significant error depends on the editor's judgment, to some extent, and so the term has become somewhat controversial. Nevertheless, the editor wishing to classify his manuscripts must adopt a meaningful notion of error. In many cases it is useful to expand the notion of error to include certain kinds of scribal innovations.

6. Insignificant Errors and Innovations

Some kinds of copying errors which turn up frequently have no value for stemma construction because they may be polygenetic; that is, they may have occurred with more than one scribe at the same point. These include a word or line out of place, a seriously misspelled word, orthographical variations, a hypometric or hypermetric line, and the omission of an occasional word or sentence.

Certain textual conditions create a situation in which a copying error is nearly inevitable for all but the most alert scribe; this kind of situation is called a *piège à copistes.* One very common trap produces the involuntary type of omission known as a *bourdon* or *saut du même au même*; it is usually not significant in stemma construction. This error occurs when the scribe's eye skips from one letter or word to an identical or similar one further on, with the result that the intervening letters or words are omitted. Thus, an abstract sequence like *ABCADE* becomes *ADE*; the letters here could represent letters, words, phrases, or lines of verse. For a concrete example of the omission of a needed syllable (*bast*), note how, in the Oxford *Roland* manuscript, a hypometric line of nine syllables,

> Si li portez cestuncel d'or mer

appears instead of the correct decasyllable, which almost certainly read:

> Si li portez cest bastuncel d'or mer.   [v. 2679]

For an example of a four-line omission due to a *bourdon*, see Part 2, VII. 7.

Two manuscripts containing the same *bourdon* are not necessarily related, unless other evidence points to a pattern in which the *bourdon* plays a small part.

The substitution of synonyms (*baron* for *segnor*) and clichés (*ains le tiers jor passant* for *ains quinsaine passant*) does not carry much weight for establishing a stemma, either. Impersonal in nature, clichés were liable to come to any scribe's mind. Nevertheless, if such substitutions are repeatedly identical in two manuscripts, instead of occasionally coincidental, they may be considered valuable evidence of relationship. For a useful list of synonyms and clichés, see Bateman Edwards, *A Classification of the Manuscripts of Gui de Cambrai's 'Vengement Alixandre'* (EM, 20; Princeton, 1926), pp. 12–24.

7. Significant Errors and Innovations

The most significant errors for stemma construction are those which bring about some kind of disharmony in the work. Some affect the sense, producing contradictory or nonsensical passages; others generate grammatical solecisms, or passages which clash with the author's usage or ideas. To detect them, the editor must have a thorough knowledge of Old French grammar and be familiar with all aspects of the author's style and cultural milieu.

Mechanical copying errors usually considered significant in classifying manuscripts include lacunas of some length and anticipation. With the latter, for example, a scribe of a verse text might anticipate the rhyme word of the second line of a couplet and substitute it for the rhyme word of the first line.

Major innovations also supply important evidence for establishing a stemma: modernization of the vocabulary, abridgment of the text, interpolations with little relation to the immediate context, and far-reaching modifications which produce a *rifacimento* or new redaction (like the rhymed *Roman de Roncevaux* compared with the older assonanced *Chanson de Roland*).

Often a constellation of variants will lead the editor to a significant error. Scribes copying a faulty text usually try to make it read coherently by correcting mistakes or filling in gaps; several scribes copying the same faulty model would probably supply different corrections for the same error. Sometimes the editor can infer from the various corrections which model the scribes were following.

8. Extra-textual Evidence

For some texts, extra-textual features of the manuscripts help establish filiations; e.g., the scribe's handwriting, the illuminations, and the other works contained in the codex. If two manuscripts are strikingly similar in these aspects, both may have been produced in the same workshop. This is apparently the case for manuscripts *A* and *D* of *Berte aus grans piés* (Paris, Arsenal 3142, and B.N. fr. 12467, respectively); see the editions by U. T. Holmes, Jr. (pp. 13–15) and Albert Henry (*Les Œuvres d'Adenet le Roi*, I, 100).

Other worthwhile evidence may be drawn from the names of patrons who commissioned the work or its copies, the owners who later acquired the manuscripts, and so on.

9. Constructing the Stemma

The stemma reproduced below was constructed by Claude Régnier for the *Prise d'Orange* (see his edition, pp. 11–13). Since his nine manuscripts (A^1, A^2, A^3, A^4, B^1, B^2, C, D, E) showed no signs of contamination, Régnier is confident that this stemma corresponds essentially to the facts of the epic's textual transmission.

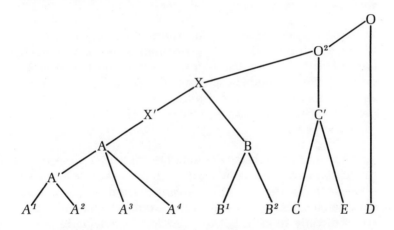

According to this stemma, the *Prise d'Orange* has come down to us in three families or redactions: X, C', and D. In turn, X gives birth to two groups, A and B, while A' heads a subgroup of two manuscripts. Régnier has edited the AB (=X) redaction, with A^1 as his basic manuscript.

Régnier gives a very clear and convincing analysis of the procedure he followed in constructing his stemma. We will summarize it step by step as an illustration of straightforward stemma construction.

Step 1. A collation of the nine manuscripts leads to a distribution into four groupings, based on additions, lacunas, and mistakes of every kind: A = A^1, A^2, A^3, A^4; B = B^1, B^2; C' = C, E; and D. Each of these groupings is characterized by style, grammar, vocabulary, and assonance or rhyme.

Step 2. The A and B groups are textually closer to each other than they are to C' or D. The C' manuscripts contain a rhymed *remaniement*, while the isolated manuscript D offers an archaic and garbled version, which Régnier thinks represents a *jongleur*'s attempt to reconstruct the epic from memory. But the A and B manuscripts contain assonanced redactions, A being a more passive version and B a revised, amplified, and modernized version of the same model. Hence, Régnier posits their descent from a common prototype X.

Step 3. X, the presumed ancestor of A and B, shares certain faults and innovations (transformed episodes, relocated *laisses*) with C'. This leads to the assumption that X and C' descend from a common ancestor O^2, which is characterized as the work of a radical reviser of the archetype (O), while D, despite its imperfections and vagaries, still comes closest to reproducing O.

Step 4. Although they belong to different families, B representatives agree frequently with C' representatives and sometimes with D. These BC'(D) agreements imply that B had a better model than A did—in other words, that A did not descend directly from X, but from some less reliable intermediary. X' stands for this intermediate copy.

Step 5. A^1 and A^2 were copied in the same scriptorium and probably had a common model, A'.

To Régnier, the choice of a basic manuscript was clear. B^1 and B^2 are eliminated because of their modernizations; A^3 and A^4 are faulty copies. This leaves the kindred manuscripts A^1 and A^2. For the *Prise d'Orange*, A^1 is superior since it contains fewer omissions and individual readings than A^2.

10. Stemma-resistant Traditions

Manuscript traditions where contamination is prevalent or where several authorial redactions may have existed will often be impossible to represent in a stemma. In such cases, the editor should attempt the usual classification; if that fails, he should try to establish groups of manuscripts even though he may not be able to determine the links between the various groups. He should in every case learn as much as possible about the tradition and the filiations of the manuscripts.

For an example of stemma construction in spite of contamination, see Rychner's Introduction to his edition of the *Bouchier d'Abevile* by Eustache d'Amiens.

11. Establishing the Text

After classifying the manuscripts to the best of his ability, the editor must decide how he will establish his text. Will he seek to approximate the author's words? Or will he present the text of a genuine medieval document with relatively little editorial interference? In making this crucial decision, he should not forget his observations about the reliability of the scribes involved, and he should also bear in mind the other options described in Chapter V of Part 1 (the controller method and manuscripts reproduced on facing pages).

For an example of choosing a basic manuscript and establishing the text and variants, see "The Birth of Alexander" in Part 3, II. 9.

12. The Method of Convergence

When an editor who desires to reconstitute the archetype of his extant manuscripts also possesses the source of his text, he may be able to converge on the archetype from both directions, with a fair amount of assurance, by comparing the extant manuscripts with the source.

For examples, see the Armstrong edition of Alexandre de Paris's *Roman d'Alexandre*, II, xvii–xxii, and Brian Blakey, "The Scribal Process," in *Medieval Miscellany Presented to Eugène Vinaver* (Manchester, Eng., 1965), pp. 19–27.

13. The Single Manuscript

When a work has survived in only one manuscript, the editor need not, of course, worry about constructing a stemma, but he should reserve his ingenuity for the task of emending which lies ahead. Without additional manuscripts, he may find it difficult to locate the errors in his base, let alone correct them.

For an example, see Peter F. Dembowski's edition of *Jourdain de Blaye*. For two radically different points of view about a single manuscript, compare Alfred Ewert's conservative edition, *The Romance of Tristran by Beroul*, which defends the manuscript text, and T. B. W. Reid, *The 'Tristran' of Beroul: A Textual Commentary* (New York, 1972), which advocates numerous emendations to approximate the original text.

14. Translation as a Controller

When the work to be edited is relatively short, the editor should envisage translating it into English or Modern French, not necessarily as part of his contemplated edition, but for the purpose of controlling the logical flow and plausibility of the basic manuscript's text. For a longer text, he might take soundings, for instance, translating its beginning, middle, and ending. A pertinent illustration of the dangers incurred by an editor overly respectful of his basic manuscript is furnished by Roques's uncompromising adherence to the Guiot manuscript of Chrétien's romances; his text proved to be intractable for a translator. When Jean Frappier translated Roques's *Lancelot*, he felt constrained, in the interests of clarity and verisimilitude, to correct the Guiot text some fifty times by drawing on the other manuscripts (*Le Chevalier de la Charrette*, pp. 13–18).

IV. WORD AND SENTENCE

1. Word Separation

Old French scribes were less conscious than we are of the limits of those language units we call words; consequently, groups of words are often run together in manuscripts. The editor must disentangle them, using the apostrophe, when necessary, to represent an elided vowel. He must also pay attention to the context, since the manner of dividing a scribal aggregate affects the sense. For example, *lauoit* might be *lavoit*, *la voit*, or *l'avoit*. Or, in the solemn scene of Joinville's *Vie de saint Louis*, when King Louis announces to his assembled barons in Acre that his mother, Queen Blanche, has urged him to return to France, the copyist of manuscript *A* transcribes the king's statement as

> ma mere ma mande . . . que ie menuoise en france.
>
> [§419]

Obviously, *menuoise* must be read *m'en voise* 'go back', not *m'envoise* 'have a good time'.

2. The Apostrophe

An apostrophe should separate elided articles and pronouns from the following word, as in Modern French: *l'on, j'ai*. It should also be used to mark the elided vowel of the possessive adjective *ma* (*m'amie*) and of composite verbs like *soi entr'encontrer*.

In twelfth-century texts, the apostrophe may signal enclitic as well as proclitic agglutinations (see Pope, §602). For example, the *ABL* version of the *Alexandre*, Alexandre de Paris's source, describes the following encounter between the Greek king and the defeated Porus:

> Porus vit Alixandre   armé sur sun destrier,
> . . . .
> Dunc lo prent per l'estref,   lo pé li vol baisier.
> Pité'n ot Alixandres   sil rova redreicer.
>   [*A*, vv. 2275, 2283–84 = Br. III, vv. 2133, 2138–39]

Here the enclitic *'n* represents *en*. However, the redactors of the two families which derived from Alexandre de Paris's *Roman d'Alexandre* dropped the enclitic *'n*, probably because it had become archaic by the beginning of the thirteenth century:

Pitié ot Alixandres . . . .   JC

Pitié en ot li rois . . . .   GM

Occasionally special circumstances preclude using the apostrophe. The quatrain which a scribe appended to the *Roman du Chevalier au Cygne* in Paris, B.N. fr. 795, offers an example:

A la fin de cest livre   ou j'ai pené jour
Voil prïer a la dame   ou toute douchors
Que deprit a son fil   doucement que tant   maint
Que me giet de pechiet   et que m'ame el ciel

[fol. 98r°]

Here the scribe wrote *maint* only once, for all four lines, and the editor should respect his verbal play, even though the third *maint* represents *m'aint* (3 pr. subj. *amer*).

3. Contractions

Most enclitic forms involving a preposition or conjunction plus a definite article or pronoun (e.g., *au, aus, des, el, es, sel, sin*) require no apostrophe once they are separated from an adjoining word. However, *del* should be divided when it is followed by a word beginning with a vowel or a nonaspirate *h: de l'enfant, de l'homme* vs. *del roi*.

Si may be a contraction representing *si + i* (adverbial pronoun), or *si + i[l]* (personal pronoun). If so, the editor should insert an apostrophe: *s'i*.

Note also the difference between enclitic *quil* (*qui + le, lo*) and proclitic *qu'il*.

4. Compound Words

A useful distinction can be established between the phrases *mes sire* or *mon seignor* and the compound *messire, monseignor*. *Mes sire* is used to refer to one's liege lord, while *messire* is a purely honorific form of polite address. Similar distinctions hold true for *ma dame* and *madame*. The case of *ma damoisele* vs. *madamoisele* rarely arises in our period (see Tobler-Lommatzsch, s.v. *damoisele*).

With compound prepositions and adverbs, as long as an editor is consistent, it matters little whether he prints *a tant* or *atant*, *a mont* or *amont*, *a val* or *aval*, *par mi* or *parmi*, etc. Certain other expressions, however, have different meanings when the elements are compounded: e.g., *de sor* and *desor*, *de sos* and *desos*, *de vers* and *devers*, *de dedans* and *dededans*. Thus, *de vers* means 'from the direction of', while *devers* has the opposite meaning of 'toward'. The compound *atot* should be written *a tot* in a text where *tot* agrees with the following noun: e.g., *a tot le bras*, *a toz ses chevaliers*, *a tote sa mesnie*, *a totes ses meschines*. (See also section 5 and Roach's note to *Perceval*, v. 7374.)

Editors often differ when they have to decide whether a verb form belongs to a compound verb. Thus, Faral regards *apaiez* as one word in Rutebeuf's *Testament de l'âne (Mais ne me tieng pas apaiez*, v. 114), while Henry chooses to print it as two words, *soi tenir a paiié(s)*, in *Buevon de Conmarchis* (see his note to v. 1416). On the other hand, the same Henry prefers *averti* (preterite) to *a verti* (past indef.) in *Berte aus grans piés*,

Son songe dist al roi,   a bien li averti,   [v. 1686]

though a similar expression in the *Alexandre* shows the use of *vertir*, not *avertir*:

"Dame, trestous les songes   doit on a bien vertir."
[Br. III, v. 7324]

Note that the line separating a fixed expression from a compound word may shift with time; thus, *avoir a faire a quelqu'un* eventually became *avoir affaire à quelqu'un*. But the editor should respect separate words in phrases which have not yet merged in Old French: e.g., *l'endemain*, *au jour d'ui*.

5. Doubled Initial and Final Consonants

One result of the scribe's running words together is the occasional doubling of a consonant which will appear at the beginning or end of a word after the editor has broken up the scribal unit. In cases where the meaning is evident, the editor may keep the doubled consonant, but if there is any doubt about the meaning, he should eliminate one of the two consonants. The following two examples will illustrate the unnecessary ambiguity which arises from retaining the scribe's spelling without modification.

In the *Sept Sages* (v. 4282), editor Jean Misrahi printed *el noussalue* as *el nou ssalue*. At first glance, this seems a misprint for *el nous salue* 'she greets us'; but, guided by the context, we see that the meaning is *el nou salue* 'she does not greet him'.

In the *Vie de saint Louis* (§190), Joinville describes how a group of explorers sailing up the Nile was watched from the banks of the river by wild beasts. Manuscript *A* reads:

Diverses bestes sauvages . . . les venoient regarder *dessus* la riviere de l'yaue aussi comme il aloient amont.

Since *dessus* here means 'from', not 'on', it should be printed *de sus*, with the first *s* deleted. Note that in this instance *riviere* retains its etymological meaning, 'riverbank'.

On the other hand, in both the following sentences from *Cassidorus*, the doubled final consonant may be retained since it does not interfere with the meaning:

Cil de la ville furent a merveilles liez, quant ill ont veü leur seigneur.   [§122]

N'enn i ot nule qui en seüst dire la verité.   [§301]

6. The Letters *j* and *v*

Although scribes make no distinction between the value of *i* and *j* or *u* and *v* (except in the case of Roman numerals), editors regularize their use according to modern orthography. Thus, *iustise* is printed *justise*.

For our period, 1150–1300, the future and conditional tenses of verbs like *avoir* are usually printed with a *v*, rather than a *u*; but for evidence of other forms, see A. T. Baker, "Le Futur des verbes *avoir* et *savoir*," *Romania*, 63 (1937), 1–30.

7. Final x

Along with final *s* and *z*, final *x* often has declensional value, serving to indicate that a word is a nominative singular or an oblique plural: *chevax* vs. *cheval*. In addition, a manuscript may offer rival forms like *chevax* and *chevaus*, a fact which explains why some editors treat *x* as if it were an abbreviation to be resolved -*ls* or -*us*. However, since one also encounters forms like *oux*, *biaux*, *consoux*, *telx*, it seems advisable to transcribe *x* as *x* in every case. (See Jean Acher, "Sur l'x finale des manuscrits," *Revue des Langues Romanes*, 56 [1913], 148–58.)

8. Expansion of Abbreviations

The numerous abbreviations in Old French manuscripts should be expanded in a critical edition. Drawing up a list of abbreviations found in the basic manuscript will help ensure consistency in resolving them. Maurice Prou's handbook, although it is devoted mostly to Latin paleography, provides a useful catalogue of abbreviations and their interpretations: *Manuel de paléographie latine et française* (4th ed.; Paris, 1924).

9. Numerals

In the past, Roman numerals in the basic manuscript (.j., .ij., .iij., etc.) have often been replaced by their spelled-out equivalents (*uns*, *dui*, *trei*), but many editors now prefer to retain the numbers as written in the manuscript, since it is not always possible to determine their precise form. This is especially true of ordinals.

10. Hyphens

In Modern French the hyphen is extensively used, but editors of Old French texts employ it only to indicate that a word has been divided at the end of a line of type. Consequently, in Old French the hyphen does not link an inverted pronoun subject to its verb in a question or an incidental clause; e.g.:

"Quen as tu fet? Ou l'as tu mis?"

[*Jeu d'Adam*, ed. Noomen, v. 731]

"Seignurs," fet il, "ore escotez!"

[*Guigemar*, ed. Ewert, v. 838]

11. Punctuation

Old French punctuation is at best haphazard and varies from scribe to scribe. Occasionally modern editors describe what they have found in their basic manuscript. While such descriptions may have historic interest, the medieval scribe's practice is usually so far removed from today's usage that it provides no guide to the syntactical structuring of the text.

Dividing an Old French sentence into the proper clauses requires close attention. In the early poetry, and even in the later prose, clauses tend to be paratactic. The editor may need to break up unending sentences by capitalizing the various connectives: *Et, Si, Mais,* etc. To elucidate the sentence's structure and meaning, he should not hesitate to use fully the resources which modern punctuation places at his disposal: comma, colon, semicolon, period, query, exclamation mark, dashes, and quotation marks.

With octosyllabic couplets, vigilant punctuation will often help clarify a difficult sentence. At other times, because of the restricted and constraining meter, punctuation seems an inadequate tool, and a textual note may be needed to explain the passage. Two examples will make this clear.

In the Oxford version of the *Folie Tristan*, Tristan asks Iseut:

"Ne membre vus quant vostre pere
Me bailla vus, et vostre mere?"

[ed. Bédier, vv. 453–54]

Here the editor has indicated by a comma that *et vostre mere* should be linked to *vostre pere*, not to *vus*.

In *Perceval*, Chrétien describes the Grail's effulgence:

Quant ele fu laiens entree
Atot le graal qu'ele tint,
Une si grans clartez i vint
Qu'ausi perdirent les chandoiles
Lor clarté come les estoiles
Font quant solaus lieve ou la lune.
[ed. Roach, vv. 3224–29]

Here punctuation provides no way to show that both *les estoiles* and *la lune* pale before the sun, and the editor must rely
on the reader's intelligence or supply a note.

12. The *Apo Koinou* Construction

In this kind of grammatically illogical double sentence, the
same phrase serves two different functions in two adjacent
clauses. Thus, for example, the object of one verb may be the
subject of another. The *apo koinou* construction occurs infrequently but is characteristic of the syntactic freedom of Old
French. To avoid misunderstanding, Henry proposed using
curly brackets to set off the phrase with a double function:

"Bien soit chascuns montés   et armés a talant,
Si verrons Malatrie   au gent cors avenant
Et les autres puceles   moult les {vois desirant}
K'avoec eles fussons   ens ou pre verdoiant."
[Adenet le Roi, *Buevon de Conmarchis*, vv. 3392–95]

13. Quotation Marks

Although French editors fail to do so, it is clearly helpful
to set off direct discourse and reported discourse by using double and single quotation marks, respectively. For example:

"Ne deüsses tu pas avoir dit: 'Ce n'est pas sanz raison
que ma damoisele m'a appelé a s'amour'? Ainssi fussez
avant alez, tot aussi que li chevaliers deüst avoir fait."
[*Cassidorus*, §117; our punctuation]

See also *Perceval*, ed. Roach, vv. 4096–140.

On the other hand, most editors adopt the French use of the dash to signal a change of interlocutor.

14. Change of Discourse

Fairly often in Old French, especially in prose narratives, discourse shifts abruptly from direct to indirect, or vice versa. For instance:

> Et il respondent que ce feront il volentiers puis que vous le comandés.
>
> [Prose *Sept Sages*, ed. Plomp, fol. 372v°]

Leo Spitzer recommended that a special mark (~) be inserted to indicate the shift (*Modern Language Notes*, 58 [1943], 134). Henry has adopted it in his edition of Adenet le Roi's poems and in his *Chrestomathie de la littérature en ancien français*; but, despite its merit, this special mark does not seem to have gained wide acceptance. Here is an example of its use in *Buevon*:

> Flandrine a Sororee   va un pou conseillant
> Et li dist que moult sont   cil chevalier sachant
> Et de bele maniere   et sage et avenant
> ~ Car pleüst a celui   en cui il sont creant
> Qu'il fussent nostre ami   tousjours a remanant,
> Car moult semblent bien estre   en tous biens entendant."
>
> [vv. 3687–92]

15. Capitals

As in Modern French, capital letters should mark the beginning of a proper name or of a sentence. Many editors also capitalize the first word of each verse, although others prefer to reserve capitals for proper names and sentence beginnings. Compare Whitehead's *Chastelaine de Vergi* with Roach's *Perceval*.

16. Exclamation Marks

The exclamation mark is used for emphasis, of course. In addition, Philippe Ménard (*Le Rire et le sourire dans le roman courtois en France au moyen âge* [PRF; Geneva, 1969], p. 474) and Jean Rychner, in his edition of *Lanval*, also employ it to warn the unsuspecting modern reader that the medieval author is being humorous or ironic. For example:

Il les unt prises par les mains:
Cil parlemanz n'ert pas vilains!   [*Lanval*, vv. 251–52]

V. DIACRITICAL MARKS

1. Use and Meaning of Diacritical Marks

Since the adoption of the Roques conventions at the Paris meeting of the Société des Anciens Textes Français in 1925, the only diacritical marks used by the editors of Old French texts are the acute accent (on the vowel *e*), the *tréma* (on the vowels *e, i* or *y, o,* and *u*), and the cedilla (under *c*).

The acute accent denotes that an *e* is stressed, i.e., that it is not mute, while the *tréma* indicates that, within a group of two or three consecutive vowels, the vowel which receives the *tréma* is not part of a diphthong or a triphthong and is to be sounded separately. The cedilla shows that a *c* is sibilant, but it has no effect on the syllabification of a word.

2. The Acute Accent

In theory, at least, editors use the acute accent to distinguish tonic *e* from atonic *e*, to avoid confusion between homographs (e.g., *celes* vs. *celés, porte* vs. *porté*), and to help the reader scan a line of verse; but it must be admitted that any one of these editorial intentions may at times run counter to some well-established convention. The following subsections explain the conventions accepted by most editors.

a. *Monosyllables.* Monosyllabic articles, demonstrative pronouns, and possessive adjectives do not take the acute accent: *les, ces* (but note disyllabic *icés*), *mes, tes, ses.* However, when the scribe drops the expected *s* at the end of *les*, a conservative editor may choose to spell it *lé*, thereby avoiding a correction. Other editors prefer correcting to *les*.

One-syllable nouns and adjectives require the acute accent on tonic *e* in the oblique singular and nominative plural, but not for forms ending in *s*. Compare *dé* 'die', *lé* 'wide', and *pré* 'meadow' with *des, les,* and *pres*.

The acute accent is used for the diphthong *ie* when it is word-final, as in *pié*, or when the following consonant is an *s*: *iés* (2 pr. ind. *estre*), *chiés*. No accent is needed when *ie* is followed by a consonant other than *s*: *chief, chier*.

b. *Polysyllables*. With very few exceptions, the acute accent in polysyllabic words is placed only on an *e* or *ie* occurring in word-final position or followed by an *s*: *abé, marchié, congiés*. When the word ends with a consonant other than *s*, no accent is needed; compare *öez* with *öés, meschief* with *meschiés*.

Exceptions where the accent is required on *ie* in nonfinal position include the disyllabic adverbs *briément* and *griément*; compare trisyllabic *liement*.

c. *Past Participles in* -ee *and* -eee. No accent is used in the case of feminine past participles: e.g., *amee, areee*. However, -ee occurring in a noun like *chasteé* or a masculine past participle of -eer verbs (*areé, beé, creé*) calls for an accent on the second *e*.

Scribes often fail to write three *e*'s in a row, despite the demands of meter and/or proper identification of a word; for example, they may not distinguish between *areee*, feminine past participle of *areer* 'to arrange', and *aree*, feminine past participle of *arer* 'to cultivate'. It is the editor's duty to restore the third *e*.

d. *Picard Past Participles in* -ie. A stumbling block which occasionally trips an editor is the Picard reduction of -iee (disyllabic) to -ie (still disyllabic), especially if the reduction affects a past participle. The editor who mistakenly views such an -ie as a Francien masculine ending (monosyllabic) and accents the *e* will produce a hypometric line in poetry and a solecism in prose. Note the syllabification of the following examples from the infinitive *laissier*:

laissié	*lais sié*	masc. p. p. (Francien and Picard)
laissiee	*lais sie e*	fem. p. p. (Francien)
laissie	*lais si e*	fem. p. p. (Picard)

e. *Past Participles in -éz, -iéz.* There are texts in which the letter z replaces final s and where at times it is difficult to distinguish between the masculine past participles in the nominative singular or accusative plural and the plural of feminine past participles. In his edition of the Old French *Pseudo-Turpin*, Claude Buridant advocates using the acute accent to indicate the masculine endings -éz and -iéz (see his p. 81). Compare, for example, masculine *departiéz* and feminine *anrichiez* in the following passage from the *Pseudo-Turpin*:

> Ces hauz saintuerez reçut [Karles] a grant joie et s'an vint a tout an France, qui puis furent departiéz aprés son decés par pluseurz leus et an furent anrichiez maintes hautes iglise[s] de France. . . .   [Prologue, 6]

Note that here *departiéz* is a declensional anomaly because it is a nominative plural masculine past participle, which does not normally require final s or z.

3. The *Tréma*

The judicious use of the *tréma* for Old French texts has long been a perplexing problem. Since the Roques conventions did not provide satisfactory guidelines for all types of cases, some editors have formulated their own rules to supplement Roques's admonitions, while others have simply followed their noses in haphazard fashion. The following subsections offer a new comprehensive guide to the use of the *tréma*: where to put it, when to use it, and when not to use it.

a. *Hiatus in a Line of Verse.* Within a line of verse, the *tréma* indicates that a mute e standing at the end of a word should not be elided with the initial vowel of the following word. Compare the different syllable values given to *Guillelme* in these lines from the *Prise d'Orange* (ed. Régnier):

> "............................
> Ne ge n'os pas la porte deffermer,
> Tant redoutons Guillelmë au cort nes." [427–28]
>
> Rois Arragon a Guillelme apelé. [569]

b. *Hiatus in Words.* Within a word, the *tréma* is used to indicate that consecutive vowels should not be considered diphthongs or triphthongs, but it is not necessary for every case of dieresis. Generally, the *tréma* is required (1) for a vowel group which was polysyllabic in Old French but has become monosyllabic in Modern French and (2) for words where confusion is possible, that is, where the reader may have difficulty identifying the word or determining its syllable count. Vowel groups which remain polysyllabic in Modern French formal prosody do not usually need the *tréma*.

Hesitation on how to scan a line of verse may arise in a score of cases. The accompanying table illustrates the *tréma*'s usefulness in distinguishing between monosyllabic and polysyllabic vowel groups and shows also which vowel in each group should receive the *tréma*. This table should not be considered exhaustive.

Vowel Groups		Examples		
ai	**vs.** a ï	pais 'peace'	**vs.**	païs 'country'
ai e	a ï e	aie 'that I have'		aïe 'help'
au	a ü	auner 'to measure'		aüner 'to assemble'
eau	ë au	beauté 'beauty'		lëauté 'loyalty'
ei	e ï	rei 'king'		reïne 'queen'
ei e	e ï e	veie 'path'		beneïe 'blessed'
eu	e ü	leu 'wolf'		leü (p.p. *lire*)
eu e	e ü e	queue 'tail'		eüe (fem. p.p. *avoir*)
iau	ï au	miaus 'better'		blïaut 'tunic'
ie	ï e	chier 'dear'		chïer 'to defecate'
ié	ï é	lié 'happy'		lïé (p.p. *lïer*)
ie e	ï e e	liee 'happy'		lïee (fem. p.p. *lïer*)

ieu	ï eu	vieus 'old'	envïeus 'envious'
iou	ï ou	ious 'eyes'	envïous 'envious'
iu	ï u	liu 'place'	Abïud (Biblical name)
oe	öe	noef 'nine'	Nöel 'Christmas'
oé	öé	oés 'need'	öés (5 pr. ind. *oïr*)
oei	ö ei	oeil 'eye'	töeil 'brawl'
oi	o ï	oir 'heir'	oïr 'to hear'
oi e	o ï e	oie 'goose'	oïe (fem. p.p. *oïr*)
ou	o ü	soul 'alone'	soüst (3 imp. subj. *savoir*)
ue	ü e	suer 'sister'	süer 'to sweat'
ué	ü é	bués 'oxen'	büés (5 pr. ind. *büer*)
ui	u ï	fui 'flee!'	fuï (p.p. *fuïr*)
ui e	u ï e	pluie 'rain'	fuïe (fem. p.p. *fuïr*)

In prose the *tréma* is, of course, not necessary for scansion, although it helps distinguish between homographs and near-homographs. However, the editor should take care not to use the *tréma* when a written vowel group may represent a single sound; for instance, in a late twelfth-century prose text, one cannot be sure whether *veu* (p. p. *veoir*) was monosyllabic or disyllabic.

    c. *Vocalic Groups Requiring Special Comment.* A number of vowel groups call for special comment.

AE: When *ae* is monosyllabic, it should be considered and printed as a double letter (a digraph): e.g., "*Savez vos ors, segnor, que vos voluns mentævre?*" (*Alexandre*, vol. I, MS *A*, v. 1583). Otherwise, the value of *ae* is disyllabic, and no *tréma* is needed.

EE: In German and English, *ee* ordinarily represents a single vowel sound: e.g., English *see*, German *die See*. Since *ee* is always disyllabic in French, no *tréma* is needed on a word like *leece*, Tobler-Lommatzsch (s.v. *lëece*) notwithstanding.

EO: In *Romania*, 52 (1926), 245 n. 2, Roques recommended the spelling *criëor* instead of the displeasing *crïëor*. Since *eo* is always disyllabic in Old French, this word should be printed *crïeor.*

IA: The *tréma* placed on the *i* by some editors seems unnecessary, there being no case of diphthongized *ia* in Old French prosody. For the treatment of *iau*, see the table above.

IE: This vowel group may be either monosyllabic (for *ié*, see section 2, a and b above) or disyllabic. When *ie* is disyllabic, the *tréma* is needed in various cases:

(a) if *ie* is preceded by one other vowel: *aïe, beneïe, oïe, fuïe;*

(b) if *ie* is followed by an n: *crïent, dïent, prïent, rïent, escïent, scïence;*

(c) if *ie* is followed by an r: *chïer, crïer, prïer, chastïer, maistrïer;*

(d) if *ie* corresponds to *iie* in the verbal suffix *-iiez.* On *-iez* vs. *-iiez,* see Whitehead's edition of the *Châtelaine de Vergy,* note to v. 318, and Buffum's edition of the *Roman de la Violette,* p. xxii.

IO: As with *ia,* one finds editors who place a *tréma* on the *i* of *io,* especially in words ending with *-ion:* e.g., *lion, Assention, fornication.* Since *io* has remained disyllabic in Modern French formal prosody, the *tréma* seems unnecessary, as Roques stated in his conventions (*Romania,* 52, 244). For the treatment of *iou,* see the table above.

OE: In *Romania,* 52, 245–46, Roques declared that editors should avoid placing a *tréma* on the first vowel of *oe* or *oé* because printers do not always have an *ö* at their disposal. This piece of advice is followed by a confusing discussion of what to do once *ö* has been rejected. Nevertheless, the simplest course is to place the *tréma* on the o: thus, *Nöel, öez, öeille.* When the o must be capitalized, the exceptional spellings *Oës* and *Oëz* seem advisable.

OO: Some English-speaking editors put a *tréma* on the second o of *oo.* However, like *ee, oo* is always disyllabic in Old French and needs no *tréma: poons* (4 pr. ind. *pooir), pooir.*

UE: Word-final *-ue* ordinarily needs no *tréma:* e.g., *drue, tondue; figue.* But there are exceptions, *eüe, agüe, argüe.*

d. *Summation.*

A should never bear a *tréma.*

E receives a *tréma* in three cases. On *e*, the *tréma* indicates (1) the nonelision of word-final *e* before the initial vowel of the following word; (2) the isolation of *e* from a following diphthong or nasalized vowel (e.g., *lëauté, jëant, lëun*); (3) the presence of a disyllabic group when the first vowel, which would normally bear the *tréma*, is capitalized (e.g., *Oës, Oëz, Uël*). Note that a capitalized vowel cannot receive a *tréma.*

I (at times written *y*) bears a *tréma* in fifteen cases: *aï, aïe, eï, eïe, ïau, ïe, ïé, ïee, ïeu, ïou, ïu, oï, oïe, uï,* and *uïe.*

O takes a *tréma* in three cases: *öe, öé, öei.*

U receives a *tréma* in six cases: *aü, eü, eüe, oü, üe, üé.*

4. Diacritical Marks in Picard Texts

Editors of texts exhibiting strong Picard traits, such as *Aucassin et Nicolette,* have had to contend with trying to convey in print what phonetic value they wished to ascribe to the letters *c* and *g.* Some of them, like Hermann Suchier and Charles Théodore Gossen, have employed the acute accent and the circumflex in special ways: *ć, ĉ, ǵ.* Others, like Roques, have been content to use only *c, ç,* and *g.*

In his edition of *Aucassin et Nicolette,* Roques wrote (p. xviii): "*c* devant *e, i,* peut représenter les sons *k* (*center, c'en* = *qu'en, civres*) ou *ts, tch, ch* (*celier, cent, cité*); nous n'avons pas distingué ces deux valeurs, comme le font les éditions de Suchier, pour ne pas ajouter à notre texte de signes diacritiques non usuels; devant *a, o, u,* il représente *k* et nous avons noté par *ç* la valeur *ts, tch, ch*; à la finale (*atenc, buc, senc, fac, siec; decauc*) un doute est possible sur la valeur du signe (*k* ou *tch*).—Le signe *g* peut de même représenter devant *e* le son *g* (*gerre*) ou le son *dj* (*gent, gist*)."

It may be argued, in favor of Roques's conservative approach, that the introduction of "signes diacritiques non usuels" tends to give the reader who is not a phonetician the feeling that he is deciphering some kind of phonetic transcription instead of reading a literary text.

VI. DIVISIONS, SUBDIVISIONS, AND NUMBERING

1. Verse Compositions

Verse compositions such as epics, most lyric poetry, and a number of didactic poems are divided by their medieval authors into *laisses* or stanzas. In this case, the editor needs only to number the *laisses* or stanzas consecutively, using Roman numerals.

Some lyric poems may demand a special stanzaic numbering in agreement with their particular structure. Thus, the triplets of Rutebeuf's *terza rima* pieces obviously call for a number opposite every third line.

Other verse compositions, especially those composed in octosyllabic verse (romances, *lais*, *fabliaux*, etc.), are usually broken up into sections of varying length in the manuscripts through the use of indentations, red and blue capitals, historiated initials, miniatures, blank spaces, and so forth. But these dividers do not necessarily go back to the poet; they can be due to the scribe or illuminator. Therefore, it is up to the editor to decide whether they provide natural, logical breaks. If so, of course he retains them. If not, he replaces them with his own way of sectioning the poem.

Numbering the lines of a poem poses at least two problems. First of all, should the editor number every fourth or every fifth line? Numbering by four and its multiples seems the better procedure, since that makes it easier for the reader to locate any line referred to in the introduction, variants, notes, glossary, and table of proper names. Next, the editor must decide on which margin of the page, left or right, he will enter his numbering. In fact, this second problem is really a double problem because it is customary to indicate in the margin also the beginning of every column of the basic manuscript: e.g., for a two-column-per-page manuscript, $1r^oa$, $1r^ob$, $1v^oa$, $1v^ob$; or 1a, 1b, 1c, 1d. Should these two vertical series of numbers appear in the same margin, where they will conflict at times, or in different margins? The decision may hinge on the edition's format. Perhaps a mock-up or layout of a specimen page could help in reaching a solution.

An additional problem arises when a text has long been read and quoted from in a well-known and respected edition. If its newest editor is led to adopt a line-numbering different from that of his predecessor, he becomes obligated to show how his own diverges from the previous editor's. Roques's solution to this problem is elegant: in his editions of Chrétien's romances, he has located his own line numbers for every two pages at the top of his right-hand page, with the corresponding Foerster line numbers in parentheses, while he placed a short synopsis in the running head of the left-hand page. Thus, for *Erec et Enide*, the headings for pages 54–55 read: "le baiser du blanc cerf" and "v. 1742–1807 (F., 1786–1855)."

2. Prose Compositions

Long prose compositions should usually be divided into chapters. When such divisions already exist in the medieval manuscript, as in the *Grandes Chroniques de France* or the *Roman de Cassidorus*, the editor should reproduce them. If no such division appears, the editor's decision to introduce one depends largely on the nature of the individual work. Any divisions should conform as nearly as possible to the work's development. Edmond Faral's nine sections, with smaller subdivisions, structure Villehardouin's *Conquête de Constantinople* in satisfactory fashion, while the 149 chapters which Natalis de Wailly superimposed on Joinville's *Vie de saint Louis* break up the text in an unnatural way.

Numbering the paragraphs throughout a prose work with Arabic numerals provides a reference framework for the textual notes. In the interest of clarity, the paragraphs should ordinarily not exceed one page in length. Some editors prefer the paragraph divisions of their basic manuscript; if these units are overlong and unwieldy, the editor may subdivide them, using letters to indicate the paragraphs established for the modern reader's convenience: e.g., §§450, 450-A, 450-B in the *Roman de Cassidorus*. Nevertheless, as with the sections in verse compositions, the scribe's paragraphs may very well represent his own work, not the author's. If the scribal divisions of the basic manuscript seem particularly inept, the author may choose to replace them.

Whereas linking variants, notes, etc., to a poem's numbered lines is an easy matter, this does not hold true when one wishes to establish this referential connection in a prose text. Should the references be to pages and lines of the edition or to small numbers or letters placed after words or sentences of the text? In the second case, how often should they start afresh? At the beginning of each chapter or paragraph? The editor of the fifteenth-century romance *Saladin*, Larry S. Crist, has numbered each sentence within a chapter, starting a new consecutive series with the beginning of every chapter, and has located these numbers in the left-hand margin of each page. In his Introduction (p. 15), he discusses the problem and the solution he has chosen.

VII. CORRECTIONS AND EMENDATIONS

Any manuscript one chooses as base will need grooming, what the French call "la toilette du texte." In addition to performing the various editorial tasks described in Chapters IV (Word and Sentence), V (Diacritical Marks), and VI (Divisions, Subdivisions, and Numbering), the editor has to identify and correct the scribe's mistakes. No manuscript is free from them.

1. Spelling

The editor must bear in mind that, in the absence of dictionaries, spelling was pretty much an affair of the scribe's own choosing, to such an extent that he often spelled the same word in different ways. When replacing words belonging to the basic manuscript with others borrowed from another manuscript, the editor should clothe the borrowings in the base's predominant spelling. This rule applies also to a short lacuna (e.g., a *bourdon*). However, when a long passage missing from the basic manuscript is to be supplied from another manuscript, the editor should make no orthographical changes in the borrowed text; he may either italicize it or indicate its length in a note.

When the scribe happens to be an extremely idiosyncratic speller, the editor should emphasize this fact in his introduction, giving appropriate examples of potentially troublesome traits. For instance, the eastern French scribe who copied *Barlaam et Josaphat* in a manuscript now at the Vatican Library (Reg. lat. 660, ed. Leonard R. Mills) exhibits a number of regional peculiarities which may perplex the unprepared reader. He wrote *es* for the second person singular present indicative of both *estre* and *avoir* (*"Por quoi es tu ce fait?"* 32.21), spelled the third person singular preterite of first conjugation verbs like *apeler* as either *apelai* or *apela*, and dropped or confused many final consonants (e.g., *tu* represents *tuit* in [*li roys*] *commandai que tu cil de sa terre venissent sacrifier as deux* 37.34f.).

For a clear presentation of one manuscript's Anglo-Norman dialectal characteristics aimed at readers familiar with Continental Old French, see "Scribal Features of MS. *H*" in Alfred Ewert's Introduction to Marie de France's *Lais*, pp. xxii–xxv.

2. Homonyms

In order to make their texts intelligible to the reader, editors usually regularize certain orthographical anomalies. Thus, they distinguish between *ce* 'this' and *se* 'if', between *ces* 'these' and *ses* 'his, her', and between *ci* 'here' and *si* 'so, and'. When the scribe blurs these distinctions, he is set right.

Nevertheless, borderline cases may arise. According to the *Vie de saint Louis* (§40), King Louis, who has narrowly escaped shipwreck, says to Joinville:

"Seneschal, ore nous a moustré Dieu une partie de son grant pooir. Car un de *ses* petiz venz, qui est si petit que a peinne le sceit on nommer, deut avoir le roy de France, ses enfans et sa femme et ses gens noiés."

Natalis de Wailly corrected *ses* to *ces*, but was he right in doing so without a textual note? One might argue that God needs only one of His least powerful winds to show His very great power. In his recent edition of the *Vie*, Noel L. Corbett maintains *ses*.

3. Final *s*

Cases of *le* for *les* and *au* for *aus* appear sporadically in thirteenth-century texts. Instead of correcting the scribe, some editors keep the *s*-less *lé* (with an acute accent) and *au*.

4. Vocalic Dissimilation

In order to distinguish *si* 'so, and' from *se* 'if', editors usually replace *se li* 'and to him, to her' with *si li*; see Whitehead's text of the *Châtelaine*, vv. 173, 635, 668. Yet other editors maintain the dissimilation; see Roach's edition of the *Perceval*, p. 365, s.v. *si* (adv.).

5. Obvious Scribal Errors

The editor should correct obvious scribal errors, including haplography, dittography, illogical word order, and omission of one of the two verses of a couplet.

At times, when a scribe notices an error of his, he will correct it as best he can. He may expunctuate letters copied wrongly or scratch something out and write anew in the cleared space; he may also write a verse or sentence that he skipped in the margin or at the bottom of the page, or insert it between two lines already written out, and use small arrows or crosses to indicate the text's proper sequence. When these corrections occur in the basic manuscript, they should be mentioned in the variants or the notes.

When the scribe omits a horizontal bar (e.g., writing *chabre* for *chābre*), the appropriate nasal consonant should usually be inserted as a correction: e.g., *chambre*. However, a spelling like *soig* or *puig* can be justified (and let stand) on the grounds that g alone may stand for a palatalized nasal, as the equivalent of *ng* or *gn*. (See Pope, §695.)

6. Less Visible Mistakes

In order to detect less obvious scribal mistakes, an editor should attempt to profile the scribe of the basic manuscript, that is, determine his weaknesses as a transcriber. For one reason or another, he may be guilty of some recurring error. Two examples may suffice.

The scribe of manuscript E of the *Second Continuation* of the *Perceval*, Roach's basic manuscript (Edinburgh, National Library of Scotland, 19.1.5), is both inattentive and at times aware of his lack of attention. When he realizes that he has strayed from his model, he attempts to patch things up as his pen moves along by rewriting the couplet he is transcribing so that it will scan properly, rhyme, and make sense locally, though it no longer fits the context. In such cases, Roach does not hesitate to intervene and bring E into agreement with the reading of the other manuscripts (see his note to vv. 30223–38, also the *First Continuation*, II, 595, note to v. 8492).

Manuscript A of Joinville's *Vie de saint Louis* (Paris, B.N. fr. 13568) is a manuscript of very small format with two narrow columns per page; the scribe must have felt cramped for space because he seems to have had trouble breaking the sentences he was transcribing into segments which would fit into his narrow columns and would still reproduce his exemplar's text accurately. This may be deduced from the large number of omissions and garbled passages of which he is guilty. Wailly (1874) and Corbett (1977) have corrected most of these with the help of the other manuscripts and the two early editions which represent lost manuscripts, but there still remain passages in A that need attention.

Here is a typical example of scribe A's omitting one small word that he should have kept. Joinville tells how a debate between Christians and Jews at the Abbey of Cluny came to naught when a knight who was present raised his crutch and felled the leading Jewish representative. According to A

La ot un chevalier a qui l'abbé avoit donné le pain leens pour Dieu. . . .

This initial reference to the knight seems satisfactory until we discover that in the other manuscripts the adjective *vieil* precedes *chevalier*; with this detail, we are immediately informed that the crutch mentioned a little later is a sign of the knight's

age, not of some injury recently sustained in combat (§§51–53).
While Wailly did not insert *vieil* before *chevalier*, Corbett did.

7. *Bourdons (Homeoteleutons)*

When a verse, or a prose sentence, starts or ends with a
word, or a group of words, identical or similar to a word or a
group of words that came shortly before, a scribe may uncon-
sciously skip the intervening passage; this is called a *bourdon*,
homeoteleuton, or *saut du même au même*. In such a case, the
editor will usually supply the skipped portion from another
manuscript, unless he wonders whether the "omitted" passage
was added to the other manuscripts, instead of having been
dropped inadvertently by the basic manuscript's scribe. Here
a proper understanding of the context is all-important.

As an example, let us consider that section of *Cligés* in
which Cligès's father Alexandre, head-over-heels in love with
Gauvain's sister Soredamors, receives a golden cup from King
Arthur as a reward for vanquishing a rebellious vassal. He then
hands the cup—not to his beloved, but to her brother! The
context shows with the greatest clarity that Chrétien is poking
fun at a young man who is at the same time a most valiant
warrior and an exceedingly timorous lover. Yet the Guiot
manuscript (Paris, B.N. fr. 794), which Alexandre Micha, the
CFMA editor, accepts as his base and follows closely, does not
include the following quatrain found in the other *Cligés* manuscripts after v. 2199, which ends with *prise*:

> La cope prant et par franchise
> Prie mon seignor Gauvain tant
> Que de lui cele cope prant,
> Mes a molt grant paine l'a prise.

In his "Notes critiques et variantes" (p. 212), Micha admits the
definite probability of a *bourdon* (i.e., the scribe's skipping
from the first *prise* to the second one), but, as a perhaps over-
cautious editor, he does not insert these four lines into his text.
So the problem of what to do in the presence of a *bourdon*
which does not run counter to the context but nevertheless
weakens the text's effectiveness remains each editor's dilemma. Will he or won't he cross the Rubicon?

8. Declensional Solecisms

Instead of the expected nominative, one not infrequently finds the oblique (or vice versa), a phenomenon obviously related to the gradual breakdown of the two-case declension. Unless the meaning of the sentence is thereby altered or obscured, it seems advisable not to correct the scribe's "error."

For example, in Whitehead's edition of the *Châtelaine*, lines 941–45 read:

> Errant se croisa d'outre mer,
> ou il ala sanz retorner,
> si devint ilueques Templier.
> Ha! Dieus! trestout cest encombrier
> et cest meschief por ce avint. . . .

In a note (p. 40), Whitehead states that he did not correct *Templier* to *Templiers* and *encombrier* to *encombriers* because the other manuscripts support the declensional error of *C*, his basic manuscript (Paris, B.N. fr. 837); their agreement leads him to infer that the archetype contained the error. He might have added that the couplet continues to rhyme, despite the solecism.

9. Prosody

An editor should, of course, pay strict attention to scansion, cesura, possible elision of final vowels, and the validity of a rhyme or assonance.

As already stated (Part 2, V. 2. c), scribes tend not to write three *e*'s in a row; it is the editor's duty to insert the missing third *e* in feminine past participles of verbs like *areer*.

During the twelfth century, and even in the thirteenth, both the decasyllabic *laisse* and the alexandrine appealed to poets as the proper molds into which to cast an epic narrative. When an editor finds an occasional alexandrine line within a decasyllabic epic, or vice versa, he should probably retain it. The decasyllabic Oxford *Roland* contains several alexandrines; for instance:

L'emperere meïsmes   ad tut a sun talent;
Cunquerrat li les teres   d'ici qu'en Orïent. [vv. 400–01]

Ço est li granz dulors   por la mort de Rollant. [v. 1437]

A conservative editor, like Bédier, is fully justified in practicing no Procrustean decasyllabification on these very acceptable dodecasyllabic lines.

On the other hand, unless there is some valid reason for not doing so, as in the above case, an editor should correct hypometric and hypermetric lines.

Intervention is also necessary if a rhyme is faulty, except when an editor faces a rare ending for which only a few words are available to the poet. *Laisse* 16 of Branch III of the *Alexandre* will illustrate this exception (vol. II, p. 150):

La ou Dayres fu mors,   tres dedevant les portes,
Les fist li rois mener   a deus de ses coortes.
Les bras en lieu d'ornicles   leur fist lïer de cordes,
Es cols leur fist lacier   les hars en lieu de torques,
Desi q'en son les forches   les fist traire a reortes.
Sor l'eaue de Gangis,   dont les rives sont tortes,
Fist les chars sevelir   des gloutons qui sont mortes.

Here, in the case of *cordes* and *torques*, we may speak of poetic license, the versifier's right to mix assonance with rhyme.

10. *Lectio Difficilior*

When the manuscripts offer two or more different readings for the same passage, editors often choose the rarer or less obvious reading, the *lectio difficilior*. The basis for their choice is the well-established rule-of-thumb that a *lectio difficilior* is more likely to represent the author's composition, whereas a *lectio facilior* could well be a trivialization of a rare reading, a banal phrase which might have occurred to several scribes independently. The certainty of the *lectio difficilior* is enhanced when the other readings can be understood paleographically as misreadings of the authentic one, or as scribal replacements for an archaic or unfamiliar word. Two examples will illustrate the concept of the *lectio difficilior*, which was formulated as early as 1697 by the classicist Jean Le Clerc in his *Ars Critica* (Amsterdam).

The prologue to the *Châtelaine de Vergy* tells how a young and valiant knight courted the Duke of Burgundy's niece with such application and solicitude that he won her love. In Whitehead's basic manuscript, vv. 18–23 read:

Si comme il avint en Borgoingne
d'un chevalier preu et hardi
et de la dame de Vergi
que li chevaliers tant ama
que la dame li otria
............s'amor.

Instead of *ama*, several other manuscripts read *pria*, a word which offers a richer rhyme than *ama* and seems to suggest that the knight observed the proper rules in his courtship. Whitehead maintains *ama* in his text and points out: "*C's ama* is the *lectio difficilior* and could easily have been replaced by *pria*, which is firmly coupled to *otria* in O.F. both by rhyme and sense. On the other hand, *ama* may be a more or less unconscious substitute for *pria*, induced by the *amor* in line 23 and the general context" (p. 31, n. to v. 21).

In the *fabliau, Du bouchier d'Abevile*, by Eustache d'Amiens, a wily butcher tries to win the *prestresse's* favors by offering her the pelt of a sheep he has stolen from the priest. For this offer, Rychner adopts the following lines in his critical edition, based on *H* (Paris, B.N. fr. 2168):

"Me pel lanue vous donrai,
Ele vaut molt de bon argent."   [284–85]

However, *lanue* appears only in manuscript *A* (Paris, B.N. fr. 837); other readings include: *Me pel amie vous donrai HT, Ma pel la fors je vos donré C*, and *Ma pel dame je vous dorrai O*. In a note (p. 91), Rychner justifies the isolated *lanue* as a probable *lectio difficilior* which has the virtue of explaining the diffraction of variants, notably *amie HT*, which he considers a misreading of *lanue*; the same could be said for *dame*. Although *lanue* is not a particularly unusual word, it is much less trivial than the common vocative *amie* or *dame*, and any scribe who replaced trisyllabic *lanue* with disyllabic *la fors* or *dame* could easily have added *je* to fill out the octosyllabic line.

11. *Locus Desperatus*

A *locus desperatus*, also called a *crux*, may be defined as a word or a passage that cannot be elucidated satisfactorily.

Perhaps the most famous of all Old French *loci desperati* occurs at the very end of the Oxford *Roland*. Line 4002 reads:

Ci falt la geste   que Turoldus declinet.

In connection with this enigmatic line, many questions arise: What is the *geste*—the source of the epic or that text itself? Is *que* a relative pronoun or a conjunction meaning *car*? Who is Turoldus, author or mere scribe? And why the Latin form of his name? Also, what is the meaning of *declinet*? Various scholars have long puzzled over these questions, but their answers, if any, have usually failed to convince their *confrères*. No one need be surprised that the ever-conservative Bédier ended his translation of the *Roland* with

Ci falt la geste   que Turoldus declinet.

When faced with a reading that resists interpretation, translation, or acceptable emendations, the editor should recognize it as a *locus desperatus* and refrain from desperate attempts to force some sense of his own on the passage. He should call it to the reader's attention in the notes.

12. Brackets and Italics

According to the convention usually observed among editors of Old French texts, square brackets indicate that a letter or a word has been added to the text, while round brackets (parentheses) tell the reader that he should subtract the letter or word they enclose. Square brackets appear more frequently than round brackets, since excised letters or words are ordinarily relegated to the variants. Some editors use italics, instead of brackets, to show that part of a word has been altered or a lacuna filled in (see Rutebeuf's *Dit des Cordeliers*, in *Œuvres*, ed. Faral and Bastin, I, 229–37).

13. Emendations

Technically an emendation, as opposed to a correction, is a change of some importance introduced into the basic manuscript text, which no manuscript nor any French and/or Latin source sanctions. Its plausibility depends on a careful study of the context and on the editor's flair. An emendation is an act of *divinatio*, especially valuable when a text is represented by a single manuscript, and a poor one to boot. For examples, see Faral's treatment of Rutebeuf's *Dit de sainte Eglise* in *Recueil de travaux offert à M. Clovis Brunel*, I, 409–21; also the Faral-Bastin edition of Rutebeuf's *Œuvres*, I, 277–85.

It must be recognized, however, that for many editors correcting and emending are almost synonymous terms.

14. Critical Texts

A critical text is more, much more, than a text critically edited. When an editor attempts not only to approximate the text of the archetype, but also to clothe this hypothetical text in the supposed language of the author, he is offering us a "critical text." This has been done repeatedly for the Oxford *Roland*, for Joinville by Natalis de Wailly, for Marie de France's *Lanval* by Jean Rychner, and for a number of other texts (see Part 1, Chapters III and V). Today, though, most editors of an approximated archetype do not change the linguistic appearance of their basic manuscript: e.g., E. C. Armstrong for the *Alexandre* and Maurice Delbouille for the *Lai d'Aristote*.

3

The Framework
of the Text

I. THE INTRODUCTION TO THE TEXT

The introduction to an edition should focus on the text
and contain only such matters as are essential for the proper
understanding and appreciation of the text. Since the texts
composed in French during the 1150–1300 period vary greatly
in nature and length, it is impossible to draw up any hard and
fast rules concerning the comprehensiveness of the introduction, the choice and order of the topics to be included, and the
amount of space to be allotted to each one.

Nevertheless, one may claim that an introduction ought to
provide information—under separate headings or not—about:
the author and date of the text; its title and contents; its literary
merit; the sources and medieval derivates; its prosody, if a
poem; the language of the author and scribe; the manuscripts;
the choice of a basic manuscript; the presentation of the text
("toilette du texte") and the editorial philosophy followed in
establishing it; previous editions, if any; and studies concerning the text.

1. The Author

For the period from 1150 to 1300, we may, in general,
classify authors into one of four groups on the basis of how
much is known about their lives: (1) anonymous writers who
remain shrouded in mystery, like the dramatist to whom we

owe the *Jeu d'Adam*; (2) anonymous writers about whom some amount of conjecturing seems legitimate, such as the poet who wrote the *Roman d'Eneas*; (3) authors for whom we know a name but precious little else, such as Rutebeuf; (4) the few named writers whose biographies are well documented outside their literary works, like Jean de Joinville.

Great caution is required for dealing with authors who fall into the first three groups. However tempting it may be, it is always dangerous to identify the romancer with the hero of his romance (e.g., Guillaume de Lorris with the narrator of the first part of the *Rose*) or to use first-person lyric poems to sketch a biography of the poet (in the case of Rutebeuf, for example).

When the author is a well-known figure, like Joinville or Jean de Meun, the editor should supply only essential facts and dates; an extensive biography is inappropriate for an edition.

2. Date

Rarely does an author of our period date his work, so the editor of an undated composition will have to determine the approximate time when it was written. He employs a pincer method for this, by trying to discover a date before which the work cannot have been written (the *terminus a quo*, or *post quem*) and a date after which it cannot have been written (the *terminus ad quem*, or *ante quem*). Then, since the gap between the *terminus a quo* and the *terminus ad quem* may be wide, the editor attempts to narrow this gap by hunting for other less widely separated dates which might be less certain than the first ones but still offer fairly probable information about the date of composition. For an example of this process of approximating the date of composition, see Alfred Foulet's edition of the *Couronnement de Renard*, pp. xxiii–xxvi.

At times scholars have been tempted to interpret a medieval piece of fiction as a *roman à clef*, a transposition of contemporary affairs into literary form. Anthime Fourrier has argued with considerable plausibility that *Cligés* reflects political events which highlighted German history during the 1170s, and his theory has been so well received that it has led to a general redating of Chrétien's *œuvre* (*BBSIA*, 1950, 69–88).

Usually, though, such attempts remain unconvincing, as in the case of the *Châtelaine de Vergy*, whose *dramatis personae* were identified by André du Chesne with Duke Eudes III of Burgundy (died 1218), his wife, and niece, while Gaston Raynaud's identifications centered on Duke Hugues IV (died 1272). In the Introduction to his edition of the *Châtelaine*, Frederick Whitehead rejects both decipherments, and for excellent reasons (pp. x–xii).

3. Title

In theory, the title given to a work should be the one selected by the author. This will usually be found within the work itself, in the prologue or epilogue. For example, Marie de France begins one of her lays very directly, with the title:

> Le lai del Fraisne vus dirai
> Sulunc le cunte que jeo sai.   [ed. Ewert, vv. 1–2]

Marie concludes another lay with its proper title and a guarantee of the story's authenticity:

> Pur l'aventure des enfaunz
> Ad nun li munz des Deux Amanz.
> Issi avint cum dit vus ai;
> Li Bretun en firent un lai.   [ed. Ewert, vv. 241–44]

For certain works which the author clearly titled, tradition has authorized another title. Thus, Chrétien's *Conte du Graal* (*Ce est li Contes del Graal*, v. 66) is often called *Le Roman de Perceval*, or simply *Perceval*, because modern readers prefer titles that name the principal character. Similarly, the author's title may have been replaced if it seemed too long for current taste and bindings. Joinville termed his biography of Louis IX "la vie nostre saint roy Looÿs" (§19); however, from 1547, date of the *editio princeps*, till very recently, it has usually been known as the *Histoire de saint Louis*. But now Noel L. Corbett, Joinville's latest editor, has chosen as his title *La Vie de saint Louis*, an acceptable twentieth-century approximation of a fourteenth-century designation.

For other medieval works, the author's short title has been lost, if indeed any ever existed. Sometimes the prologue provides a summary of the episodes to be narrated, perhaps in lieu of a title. For example, Lambert le Tort's Alexander romance has not survived in its original form, yet its contents may be guessed from the following *laisse*:

> De Daire lo Persant   qu'Alixandres conquist,
> De Porus lo rei d'Inde   qu'il chaiça et ocist
> E des bones Arcus   que il cercha et quist
> E de la fort citté   Babiloine qu'asist
> E de la voiz des arbres   qui de sa mort li dist
> E si cum Apelés   s'image contrefist,
> De Got et de Magot   que il enclaust et prist,
> Que ge mais n'enn istrunt   trosqu'au tens Anticrist,
> Del duc de Palatine   qu'il pendi et ocist
> E si cum Aristotes   l'entroduist et aprist,
> La verté de l'estoire,   si cum li reis l'escrist,
> Uns clers de Chasteldum,   Lamberz li Torz, la fist,
> De latin o el ere   qui en romanz la mist.
>
> [*Roman d'Alexandre*, VI, 88]

Whatever title Lambert may have chosen for his poem is beyond surmise. For practical reasons, though, the editors of the *Roman d'Alexandre* have entitled it *Alexandre en Orient*.

In some cases where the author gives no title, a scribal rubric or *explicit* in a manuscript may supply one, as with *Aucassin et Nicolette*, where the rubric in the unique manuscript reads "C'est d'Aucasin et de Nicolete." The editor should keep in mind, however, that the rubric and *explicit* were probably not composed by the author.

After determining a title, the editor must decide on its orthography and morphology: will he retain the Old French forms or adopt modern ones? For example, he must choose between *Le Couronnement Looÿs* and *Le Couronnement de Louis*, between *La Chastelaine de Vergi* and *La Châtelaine de Vergy*, between *Cleomadés* and *Cléomadès*. Most editors today favor Modern French forms for the title, especially if the title is the editor's choice, rather than the author's. But even an editor who keeps Old French forms in the title will use the modern spellings (e.g., Cléomadès, Cligès) when referring to the eponymous protagonist in his introduction or notes.

Modernization occasionally leads an editor to rephrase a title in order to substitute a current word for one which has disappeared from the language. This is the case for Renaud de Beaujeu's Li Beaus Desconeüs, which has become Le Bel Inconnu.

4. Summary of Contents

The summary should be concise, yet relatively detailed, with precise references to the text (laisses, stanzas, or verses of poems; chapters or paragraphs of prose compositions). It should enable the reader to form an idea of the plot, structure, and principal themes of the whole work, or to relate a passage he may wish to study to what has come before and what will follow. For instance, a helpful summary of Chrétien's Perceval will include the adventures of both Perceval and Gauvain.

5. Literary Evaluation

The editor of the Oxford Roland, of Chrétien's Yvain, or of Aucassin et Nicolette need not tell us that the work in question is a masterpiece, although he may wish to compare it with other outstanding works in the same genre. Works of lesser stature, however, may usefully be evaluated in terms of modern taste, with all due allowance for the fact that the medieval esthetic perspective differs from ours in such matters as love of allegory and annominatio and accounts of jousts and tourneys. Disparaging assessments like "second-rate" or "third-class" are invidious, but a serious attempt to characterize the edited work in more neutral terms (second rank, third level, fourth group, etc.) will be welcomed by many scholars. Neither editor nor reader should regard a statement that a given work belongs to a literary third group as a condemnation of it or of the editor for having chosen to edit it. Conversely, the editor should beware of overrating a work on which he has lavished time and effort in the editing process.

6. Sources

When the author of a text has clearly been influenced by earlier works in Latin or Old French, the introduction should cite these sources. Textual evidence of sources is best confined to the notes. However, if textual evidence from a source helps establish the correct text of a passage, this fact should be mentioned in the introduction.

The use of a Latin source is, of course, a clue to the writer's social condition: he is presumably a cleric, or at least someone who has received clerical training.

7. Derivations and Continuations

A text may influence subsequent compositions in a number of ways—most directly by giving rise to adaptations and modernizations of itself and by generating sequels or cycles. The introduction should name those derivations which are textually linked to the edited work, including any Middle French *remaniements* and reworkings in other European languages. The *Roman d'Eneas* offers a good example of a text with wide-reaching influence.

8. Versification

Under the heading of versification, the editor should describe the poet's handling of meter and rhyme: with decasyllabic and dodecasyllabic lines, the grammatical appropriateness of the cesura; with octosyllables, the relation between rhymed couplet and sense, the freedom of the lines, the frequency of enjambment; in general, the variety of assonances or rhymes, the use of unusual words, and poetic license for irregular rhymes. An analysis of this sort will inevitably lead to some assessment of the poet's competence and to an appreciation of the stylistic level of his verse.

Discussion of occasional blemishes such as imperfect rhymes or declensional infractions due to the scribe should be relegated to the notes (see Part 2, VII. 9).

For works with particular lexicographical interest, the editor may wish to compile a table of the poet's assonances or rhymes; it might help the reader find words which were not obscure enough to be listed in the glossary. If these assonances or rhymes are numerous and the table exceeds, say, a page or two, it should form an appendix, rather than disrupt the flow of the introduction.

9. Language of the Author

In the absence of the author's holograph manuscript, only the language of the scribe can be thoroughly analyzed, the language of the author but thinly transpiring through it in the manner of a palimpsest. For a rhymed work, the words used at the rhyme are the surest guide to the poet's phonology, since scribes tended generally to respect the rhymes. Thus, rhymes of etymological -ie endings with feminine -ie (= reduction of -iee), such as chevalerie : ensauchie (fem. p.p. modifying chevalerie) in the Couronnement de Renard, vv. 1–2, may indicate Picard traits in the author's dialect. The meter may also furnish some pointers; for instance, the extra syllable in the svarabhactic future and conditional forms (avera vs. avra, averoit vs. avroit) is also a Picard trait. However, the conventional literary language of Old French, the koine, tolerated a variety of dialectal traits as a kind of poetic license, so unless these traits are numerous and fairly regular, they do not provide a reliable clue to the author's dialect.

10. Language of the Scribe

Although the scribe's language lends itself to thorough analysis, as noted above, the editor should point out to the reader only the essential characteristics which allow the correct localization of the scribe's dialect, and any idiosyncrasies in grammar and spelling which may cause difficulties in reading. There is no need to duplicate the descriptions of Old French and its various dialects given in the standard manuals of Schwan-Behrens, Pope, Gossen, L. Foulet, Ménard, Moignet, and Raynaud de Lage.

Morphological, lexical, and orthographical signs of modernization by a Middle French scribe include: breakdown of the two-case declension, which most authors observed up to the end of the thirteenth century (considerably later in Picardy); giving a feminine ending to an adjective which previously had the same form for both genders, e.g., grande; adding a final -e to the first person singular of the present indicative, e.g., j'aime; replacing an archaic or obsolescent word with a Middle French neologism, e.g., mout by beaucoup; and the use of Latinized spellings like debvoir and sçavoir.

11. Manuscripts

Here the editor should list all the manuscripts and fragments of the work to be edited, in the alphabetical order of their sigla, with manuscripts first and fragments afterwards. The minimum information given for each should include the present library location, current shelf number, and date or approximate date. If a manuscript has been described in detail elsewhere, the editor should refer the reader to that description.

In the case of the basic manuscript, particularly if the manuscript is not well known or has not been accurately described, the editor may wish to provide a full bibliographical description. This will include the following facts: surface material (vellum or paper); dimensions in millimeters; number of folios occupied by the work, with *incipit* and *explicit*; total number of folios; number of columns per page; number of lines per column; ornamentation (capitals, miniatures, full-page illuminations); changes of scribal hand, if any; other works contained in the codex, with precise folio references for each; construction (regular or irregular assemblage of quires, blank pages, etc.); binding (material, style, date, provenance); history of the codex (former owners, bookplates, appearance in library or sale catalogues, former shelf numbers); microfilms and photocopies available in private and public libraries.

For examples of both brief and full descriptions, compare Roques's list of the manuscripts containing *Erec et Enide* with his detailed account of the Guiot manuscript (CFMA edition, pp. xxviii–xxxi and xxxvii–xliii).

12. Choice of the Basic Manuscript

The editor should explain how he has classified his manuscripts and divided them into families, groups, and subgroups. His discussion will cite some readings which substantiate his classification and, perhaps, others which his classification fails to explain. A stemma could illustrate this discussion. Good examples of manuscript classifications and stemmas may be found in Claude Régnier's edition of the *Prise d'Orange*, Duncan McMillan's edition of the *Charroi de Nîmes*, and Jean Rychner's edition of Eustache d'Amiens's *Bouchier d'Abevile*.

When no stemma can be constructed, the editor should give his reasons for choosing his basic manuscript and controllers.

13. Establishment of the Text

Here the editor should sum up his editorial philosophy concisely and explain how and why he has intervened in the text. He should make clear the relationship between his edited text and the basic manuscript or its presumed archetype. In particular, he should state how he has modified his basic manuscript: resolution of abbreviations, treatment of Roman numerals and the letter x, normalization, corrections, and emendations; punctuation, diacritical marks, brackets, and italics; paragraphs, sections, chapters, line numbers; handling of variants, notes, and appendixes.

14. Bibliography

A serviceable bibliography should list: (a) previous editions; (b) medieval adaptations in other languages, if published; (c) modern translations; (d) monographs and articles, and occasionally reviews, in which the text has been analyzed and discussed.

To delineate previous editions, some brief analytical comment is helpful: basic manuscript; merits and failings of the edition; and important critical reviews of it. For well-known and often-printed works, like the *Roland* or Joinville's *Vie de saint Louis*, only the major editions need be mentioned.

Except in the case of texts edited for the first time, the bibliography of literary studies should be selective, especially for the period covered by the standard bibliographies of Bossuat and Cabeen-Holmes.

II. THE CRITICAL APPARATUS

1. Variants vs. Rejected Readings

In its broadest meaning, the term *variant* refers to any manuscript reading which differs from the constituted text of the edition. More precisely, a *variant* is a reading found in a manuscript other than the basic manuscript and different from the text of the edition, while any reading of the basic manuscript which the editor has seen fit to correct or emend is called a *rejected reading*. Together, the variants and rejected readings make up the *critical apparatus* of the edited text. Sometimes the collective term *variants* is used interchangeably with *critical apparatus*; however, a critical apparatus consisting only of readings rejected from the basic manuscript should not be labeled "Variants."

2. Purpose of the Critical Apparatus

The critical apparatus should allow the reader to reconstruct the exact text of the basic manuscript, including errors and scribal corrections (e.g., expunctuations); therefore, it must give every single rejected reading. When several manuscripts are involved, the apparatus should also permit the reader to assess for himself the value of the manuscripts besides the basic one and of the editor's recension; hence, it must list fairly complete variants for each line of verse or each sentence of a prose text.

Still another function of the critical apparatus is to inform the reader about changes in the number of witnesses to the text. When a section of the text is missing in one or more of the manuscripts, the editor should signal the precise extent of the gap in the apparatus; otherwise, the reader will assume that all manuscripts furnishing variants are complete at this point and that the unlisted manuscript or group of manuscripts sides with the basic manuscript against the dissenting witnesses in cases where the reading remains uncertain.

3. Choosing the Variants

How complete the variants should be depends on a number of factors: primarily, the nature of the text, the number of manuscripts, and space limitations imposed by the general editor of a series. Ordinarily the variants need not include unimportant dialectal or orthographical variations, minor changes in word order, or insignificant errors committed by scribes other than the basic one.

For texts represented by a large number of manuscripts, the editor will inevitably have to narrow his choice of variants even more. He should, of course, list all rejected readings. In addition, he should supply the variants which pertain to obscure or corrupt passages in his basic manuscript and those which have enabled him to classify the manuscripts into groups and families. Beyond this, however, he will be obliged to sacrifice many other significant variants that he would normally include: for instance, words or phrases of lexicographical interest which do not appear in his base and proper names of historical or geographical importance which are likewise absent from the basic manuscript.

4. Location of the Critical Apparatus

Variants and rejected readings may be placed at the bottom of the page containing the printed text or, if they are too numerous to be so located, in a special section following the entire text. For purposes of checking and control, it is far easier to consult a critical apparatus which appears at the bottom of each printed page of the text.

Two recent editions provide good models of this type of variant placement: Régnier's edition of the *Prise d'Orange* and McMillan's *Charroi de Nîmes*. In both these editions, the rejected readings and variants are presented in two separate clusters, the rejected readings coming first. The more traditional procedure is to group the rejected readings and variants together, with the variants following the rejected readings for each line. See section 9 below for an example of choosing variants and arranging the critical apparatus in a single block.

5. Presentation of Variants

In a single-section critical apparatus, these conventions obtain: the line number (or prose sentence number) precedes the variants for each verse or prose sentence; it is followed by the siglum of the basic manuscript (if there is a rejected reading), the rejected reading, then a comma. Next come the divergent readings from the other manuscripts, preferably in the alphabetical order of their sigla, with commas between readings. It is, of course, perfectly permissible to place the siglum or sigla after each reading instead of before it. All sigla should be italicized, as should all editorial comments (e.g., *adds, omits, sic, +1, −1*). A dash signaling the end of the variants for one verse precedes the number of the next verse.

If the rejected readings from the basic manuscript are listed in a separate section, they do not have to be preceded by the basic manuscript siglum, but the comma and dash should be used, as just described, to indicate necessary distinctions between variants.

Whenever a variant or rejected reading in a poem is metrically incorrect, the editor should indicate this with (+1), (+2), etc. for a hypermetric line (too many syllables) or (−1), (−2), etc. for a hypometric line (too few syllables).

If two manuscripts offer the same variant reading, with only minor orthographical differences between them, the editor should list their reading just once, accompanied by the sigla of both manuscripts in alphabetical order. He will ordinarily adopt the spelling of the first manuscript cited. For instance, the two nearly identical variants of the *Bouchier d'Abevile* at v. 284, *Me pel amie H* and *Ma pel anmie T*, call for a joint listing: *Me pel amie HT*.

A variant which exceeds a reasonable length (e.g., an interpolation of twenty lines) should be relegated to an appendix if it is interesting enough to be included in the edition.

6. Styling the Variants

For the "toilette" of the variants and rejected readings, editors usually observe the following conventions:
    a. separate words, as in the text;
    b. distinguish *j* from *i* and *v* from *u*;
    c. capitalize words and add diacritics, as in the text;
    d. do not supply punctuation, since a comma separates variants within the same verse or prose unit and a period marks an abbreviation.

7. Anchoring the Variants

Indicate clearly where each variant departs from the edited text. If the variant begins with the first word of a line or sentence, capitalize the first letter, if this is done in the text. If the variant substitutes one noun, proper name, adjective, verb, or adverb for another with the same number of syllables (e.g., *roi* for *duc*, *bon* for *bel*, *l'a mort* for *l'occist*), the identity of syntactic function and similarity of meaning will usually show where the variant appears in its manuscript, and the variant may be listed by itself.

However, when the reader may have trouble determining where the variant fits into the text, the editor should denote its context unambiguously by supplying the preceding or following word, or both. Also, if the variant resembles an entire line of the text but contains several changes, as in v. 4 of manuscript B in the *laisse* edited below, the editor may wish to cite the whole line in abbreviated form.

When it is necessary to repeat a word which occurs in both variant and text, abbreviate any such word that has three or more letters (see section 8).

8. Abbreviations

To minimize the size of the critical apparatus, editors nearly always abbreviate words which are the same in the constituted text and the variants, but this may lead to confusion, so the editor should exercise prudence here. For the sake of clarity, it is probably wise not to abbreviate two-letter words: e.g., *as, de, du, en, es, et, eu, fu, il, je, la, le, li, ma, me, ne, se, si, ta, te, tu*. For words more than two letters long, usually the first letter followed by a period will be a sufficient abbreviation. Abbreviating words of this length not only saves space, but also calls attention to those words which are printed in full— the true variants.

When a word starts with a different initial in text and variant (e.g., *iert* in text vs. *ert* in variant), the initial from the text should be used for the abbreviation of the variant (*i.* for *ert* in our example).

When a variant word differs in case or number from its form in the text, it should probably not be abbreviated.

9. "The Birth of Alexander": Text and Critical Apparatus

The following passage on the birth of Alexander the Great, with its comments and critical apparatus, illustrates many of the procedures involved in preparing a critical edition which we have discussed in Part 2.

Laisse 2 of the *Alexandre décasyllabique* (*Alexandre*, III, pp. 61–62) has come down to us in three manuscripts:

A (Paris, Arsenal 3472) 11 decasyllabic verses, printed in *Alexandre*, I, p. 2;

B (Venice, Museo Civico Correr VI, 665) 12 decasyllabic verses, printed in *Alexandre*, I, p. 3;

L (Paris, B.N. fr. 789) 11 alexandrines, printed in *Alexandre*, III, p. 104.

In addition, the readings of *A*, *B*, and *L* have been collated with the text of Alberic de Pisançon's *laisse* 7 (vv. 46–53, *Alexandre*, III, p. 39), since this octosyllabic text served as the decasyllabic poet's source.

These four texts are transcribed below without punctuation, but with the benefit of diacritical marks.

Alberic
Reys Alexander quant fud naz
Per grant ensignes fud mostraz
Crollet la terra de toz laz
4 Toneyres fud et tempestaz
Lo sol perdet sas claritaz
Per pauc no fud toz obscuraz
Janget lo cel sas qualitaz
8 Que reys est forz en terra naz

A
Quant Al'x.   li filz Felips fu nez
Per molt granz signes   fu li jors demostrez
Li ceus mua   totes ses calitez
4 Seleil e luna   perdirent lor clartez
Por poi ne fu   li jors toz oscurez

Crolla la terre   e se mut de tot lez
En plusors los   fu granz la tempestez
8 Li reis Felis   fu molt espaventez
De cel enfant   qui si fu demostrez
Ce signifie   qu'il sera molt senez
E que li enfes   conquerra mainc regnez

B

Quand Al'x.   li filz Felipes fu nez
Par mout grand signes   fu li rois demostrez
Li ciels mua   totes ses qualitez
4 Li soloil e la lune   perdirent ses clartez
Li jors meesmes   torna en escurtez
Croloit la terre   si trembloit de toz lez
En mer profunde   fu grans la tempestez
8 Li rois Felipes   fu mout espoantez
De cel enfant   que si fu demostrez
Ce senefie   que il ert mout senez
E que li enfes   conquerra maint regnez
12 Les amirauz   e totes les citez

L

Quant Alixandres fu   li fius Phelippe nes
Par mout grans signes fu   icel jour demostrés
Car li cius en mua   toutes ses qualités
4 Li solaus et la lune   perdirent lor clartés
Et li jours si en fu   durement oscurés
Forment croissi la tere   environ de tous les
En mer parfonde fu   mout grans la tempestés
8 Li rois ses pere en fu   forment espöentés
Por l'enfant ki fu nes   s'iert li signes mostrés
Ce fu senefianche   k'il seroit mout senés
Et que il en sa vie   conkerroit maint regnés

Since *L* presents an alexandrine reworking, the choice
of a basic manuscript lies between *A* and *B*. *A* is preferable to
B for the simple reason that it has been transcribed by a Poi-
tevin scribe, whose dialect is the same as that of the decasyllabic poet. In addition, at least for *laisse* 2, *A*'s text calls for
fewer corrections than *B*'s, were *B* to be the base. *B* has two
hypermetric readings (vv. 1 and 4); *grand* in v. 2 does not agree
with *signes*, and *rois* is less apposite than *jor(s)* in *AL*; *ses* for
lor in v. 4 is a dittography caused by *ses* of v. 3; *B*'s text of v.

5 diverges overmuch from that of *A, L,* and Alberic; its twelfth
line finds no backing in *A, L,* and Alberic.

A's text needs to be corrected in four instances. In v. 2
Alixandres is meant to be the subject of *fu . . . demostrez;* therefore, *li jors* should be changed to *lo jor.* In v. 4 *Seleil* is an
obvious lapsus calami for *Soleil;* in v. 6 a correction of *de tot
lez* seems called for by the *toz oscurez* of the preceding line.
In v. 7 *En plusors los* does not fit the context: the portents
which embrace the sky (vv. 3–5) and the earth (v. 6) demand
a mention of the sea in v. 7, as in *B* and *L.* The spelling *per-
funde,* vs. *B profunde* and *L parfonde,* is authorized by *A,* v.
2460: *Lunc la rive de l'aiqua   est si perfunz li bez.*

Borderline cases occur in vv. 1, 4, and 11. In v. 1 *Felips*
looks more like a nominative than an oblique, while in v. 4
Soleil presents us with the opposite phenomenon. Since the
meaning is clear and the meter correct in each instance, *Felips*
(instead of *Felip*) and *Soleil* (instead of *Soleiz*) have been allowed to stand. In v. 11 *A*'s *mainc* is just as acceptable as *BL*'s
maint, vs. the more grammatical *mainz.*

The edited text follows.

> Quant Alixandres,   li filz Felips, fu nez,
> Per molt granz signes   fu lo jor demostrez:
> Li ceus mua   totes ses calitez,
> 4 Soleil e luna   perdirent lor clartez,
> Por poi ne fu   li jors toz oscurez,
> Crolla la terre   e se mut de toz lez,
> En mer perfunde   fu granz la tempestez.
> 8 Li reis Felis   fu molt espaventez
> De cel enfant   qui si fu demostrez.
> Ce signifie   qu'il sera molt senez
> E que li enfes   conquerra mainc regnez.

Critical Apparatus:
2—1 B Felipes (+1), L Phelippe—2 A li jors, B li rois, L icel j.—
4 A Seleil, B Li s. e la l. p. ses c. (+2)—5 B Li j. meesmes torna en
escurtez, L Et li j. si en fu durement o.—6 A de tot l., B Croloit la t.
si trembloit de t. l., L Forment croissi la t. environ de t. l.—7 A En
plusors los—10 B que il ert, L k'il seroit—11 BL maint—11.1 B Les
amirauz e totes les citez

III. THE NOTES

1. Location

Ideally, textual notes should be located at the bottom of the pages containing the text they annotate, below the variants. Unfortunately, this arrangement is rarely feasible, and the notes usually constitute a separate section following the text, but preceding the table of proper names and the glossary.

When the notes are not too numerous, the editor may mark the passages elucidated therein with an asterisk in the text; this would help the reader, who otherwise has to follow two sequences in different parts of the volume.

2. Primary Functions of Notes

The notes serve two main purposes: justifying the text which the editor has established and explaining textual difficulties to the reader.

Under the heading of justification, the editor should give his reasons for accepting a reading or punctuating in a certain way whenever it seems likely that other readers might fail to understand his decision or might challenge it. When he is unsure about the text—in the case of a *locus desperatus* or *lectio difficilior*, for example—he should frankly admit his doubts.

Explanatory notes should help the reader with difficult passages. They provide information about grammatical or lexical problems, meters and rhyme; and frequently they supply translations to aid in interpretation. If the passage is unintelligible, the editor should say so. In deciding which grammatical features require explanation, the editor must make certain assumptions about the background of his readers. It should not be necessary to draw attention to the basic characteristics of Old French, such as the two-case declension.

3. Notes for Commentary

In addition to their primary functions, the notes may provide further information about the text: its Latin or Old French sources, analogues in contemporary works, or imitations. The editor may also discuss the historical or cultural background of a passage and comment on the author's style.

Recently some editors have divided their notes into two separate sections: "Critical and Explanatory Notes," followed by "Historical and Literary Commentaries" (see *Le Roman de Renart, Branches I et Ia*, ed. N. Fukumoto). This distinction, useful in planning the notes, serves in practice only to complicate the reader's task, for he now has to flip back and forth from text to notes to commentaries in order to ascertain the editor's point of view and share his knowledge about the text. When the notes must follow the text, they are easier to consult in a single section.

4. Brevity

The editor should aim for extreme concision in his notes. If his discussion of a certain item (a word, construction, etc.) exceeds a page or so in length, he ought to consider relegating it to an appendix.

IV. THE GLOSSARY

1. Scope

Nineteenth-century editors often compiled complete glossaries, but today, for most texts, a partial or selective glossary is sufficient. However, a text which is relatively short, of superior quality, and of marked lexical interest may still warrant a full glossary, such as the excellent one provided by Albert Henry in his edition of Jean Bodel's *Jeu de saint Nicolas*.

An editor preparing a selective glossary must carefully balance his inclusions against his exclusions. Despite his care, readers will almost inevitably criticize him for glossing words which cause them no difficulty and for leaving out others which they would have defined. A statement explaining the editor's principles of selection might introduce the glossary.

2. Inclusions

To choose entries for the selective glossary, the editor should first single out words which have perplexed him, words he had to look up in Godefroy or Tobler-Lommatzsch. Then he should add words which he may know but which could puzzle a reader less familiar with the dialectal traits of the text, the idiosyncratic spellings of the basic manuscript, or the technical aspects of the subject matter. He should also seek out those words or expressions which would seem perfectly intelligible to many readers, yet have different meanings from their modern ones. For example, in the twelfth and thirteenth centuries, *sinople* means 'red', not 'green', and *faire semblant* means 'express visibly', but not necessarily 'feign'. A somewhat different case is illustrated by the use of the word *chevalier* in *Les Faits des Romains*, an Old French translation of the *De Bello Gallico* from ca. 1214; there Cæsar's *milites* (legionaries, foot soldiers) frequently appear as *chevaliers*. This denomination may at first surprise the modern reader until he remembers, or is reminded, that in medieval Latin documents a knight is called *miles*, not *eques*.

In addition to entries culled from the edited text, the glossary should include unusual words or forms which appear in the rejected readings and variants.

While in the early stages of gathering material for the glossary, the editor should make note of all occurrences of potential entries, though he usually will not list all line or paragraph references in his final version.

3. Exclusions

Formulating a consistent policy of exclusions is perhaps more difficult than determining which words to include because it leads to rules which constrain the editor unnecessarily. In his SATF rules, Roques recommended that editors exclude words which were satisfactorily defined in a standard compendious dictionary—the Petit Godefroy then, today possibly Greimas. Readers of Old French texts presumably have such a dictionary at hand. However, a one-volume dictionary cannot illustrate words with enough examples to show the range of their meanings and use, so the editor should regard Roques's precept as a rule-of-thumb, rather than an iron-clad requirement. The audience for whom the edition is intended also influences the scope of the glossary.

4. Lexical Indexes

Besides a glossary, some texts warrant a separate table of words belonging to a specialized vocabulary. Thus, Henry's glossary of the *Jeu de saint Nicolas* is followed by an "Index méthodique du vocabulaire de la taverne, du vin, des dés, de l'argent." Since the picaresque element is so strong in Bodel's comedy, the index serves a useful purpose by drawing the reader's attention to words spoken in an Arras tavern.

Less closely related to the text are the tabulations of words found in Roques's CFMA editions of Chrétien's romances and the various branches of the *Roman de Renart*. In additon to a normal glossary, he provides an analytical survey along physical, social, and cultural lines. Words are divided into four main categories: "Vie matérielle; Institutions; Sciences, arts et techniques; Usages et dictons." Each category features several subgroups. This kind of lexical inventory is probably more useful to the social historian or the lexicographer trying to define courtly and noncourtly levels of Old French than to the reader interested in medieval romances and other literary topics.

5. Form of Glossary Entries

The editor should examine with care the formal layout of the glossary in several reputable editions, such as those by Henry or Roques. The recommendations below call attention to some of the basic procedures of arrangement and economy.

a. *Alphabetizing*. Nouns, pronouns, articles, and adjectives are alphabetized by their singular oblique (accusative) case forms, with the exception of personal pronouns, whose main entry is customarily the nominative case form, e.g., *je, tu, il*.

Verbs are usually listed under the infinitive form. Infinitives of reflexive verbs should be followed by *soi*, not *se*, or *s'*, unless an abbreviation like *refl.* is preferred: *adober (soi), dementer (soi).*

Cross references to main entries may prove useful: e.g., *ber* to *baron*, *maire* to *maior*, *roiamant* to *raembre.*

When the form used for the main entry does not occur in the basic manuscript, it should be enclosed in square brackets.

b. *Special Symbols.* Entries discussed in the notes should be followed by an asterisk.

Words occurring at the rhyme may be designated by (:) if there exists some possibility that they are ad hoc creations whose sole purpose is to provide a suitable rhyme. This is, in all likelihood, the case of the hapax legomenon *amoronge* in *Yvain* (ed. Roques):

> Mes tost deïst, tel i eüst,
> que je vos parlasse de songe,
> que la genz n'est mes amoronge
> ne n'ainment mes, si con il suelent,
> que nes oïr parler n'an vuelent.   [vv. 5386–90]

Of the eight *Yvain* manuscripts, only one, Roques's basic manuscript, has *amoronge*, while all the others, which presumably reflect Chrétien's text here, read:

> que je vos parlasse d'oiseuse
> car la janz n'est mes amoreuse.

Nevertheless, Tobler-Lommatzsch not only lists *amoronge*, but actually provides it with a nonattested masculine form: *amoroin!*

Entries drawn from the variants should be identified by *v.* or *var.*, or by the sigla of the manuscripts from which they come when more than two manuscripts are involved.

When a text contains a passage borrowed from another author, any word which appears in the insert might profitably be marked. Thus, the *Vie de saint Louis* contains two long passages which were bodily lifted from some manuscript of the *Grandes Chroniques de France* (§§692–729, 739–54 + 758–

59); references to words found in these passages could be indicated by *GC*.

c. *Abbreviations*. It is customary to make the grammatical identifications of words as brief as possible: e.g., 6 *pr. ind.* for third person plural of the present indicative. Abbreviations used for this purpose vary, but whatever system the editor adopts should be made clear to the reader. Many editors place a key to their abbreviations and symbols at the head of the glossary.

d. *Textual References*. When a word to be entered in the glossary occurs frequently in a text of any length, the editor ordinarily needs to provide only a few textual references, citing the first two or three occurrences.

e. *Typefaces*. Usually the glossary entry and its line numbers from the text are in roman type while the identifying symbols and definitions are in italics.

6. Elliptical Sentences and Grammatical Identifications

When providing grammatical identifications, the editor should keep in mind the elliptical nature of much Old French poetry, especially that written in octosyllabic couplets. Two examples will be of interest here, one taken from the *Châtelaine de Vergy*, the other from the *Lai d'Aristote*:

Morte se tient et a despite.   [ChV 662]

L'uns est de mesdire entremetre.   [LA 25]

Both lines give a dual role to a preposition; in addition, *LA* 25 omits the reflexive pronoun. In grammatical prose ChV 662 becomes

A morte se tient et a despite,

and *LA* 25 calls for

L'uns est de soi entremetre de mesdire.

It follows that in a glossary the verbs *tenir* and *entremetre* should appear as *tenir (soi) a* and *entremetre (soi) de*. Note that in a Modern French expression like *envoyer promener quelqu'un*, *promener* is implicitly reflexive in the same way.

7. Definitions

If the contextual meaning of a word seems rather distant from its basic meaning, the glossary might offer both definitions. For example, at vv. 80–81 of the Berne *Folie Tristan*, Tristan says of the absent Iseut:

> "Encor avroie je mout chier
> S'a li me pooie acointier."

Bédier helpfully glossed *acointier* as 'entrer en rapports avec; rejoindre'. 'Rejoindre', though correct for this context, would not be an adequate definition since *acointier* does not ordinarily have that meaning.

V. THE TABLE OF PROPER NAMES

1. Location

The table of proper names either precedes or follows the glossary.

2. Contents

All proper names should be entered, including those familiar to every reader, like *Deus*, *Nostre Dame*, and *Paradis*, and all allegorical figures, such as *Amour*, *Biauté*, and *Nature*.

For certain works the concept of *proper name* should be expanded to embrace anonymous characters, like the unnamed principals of the *Lai de l'Ombre*, the nameless damsels and knights of Chrétien's *Lancelot*, or the lion of *Yvain*. Note that Roques calls his table of proper names for *Lancelot* an "Index des noms propres et des personnages non dénommés."

3. Form of Entries

Proper names should be listed in their oblique form. If the name does not occur in this form, it should be entered in a form used by the author (nominative or vocative case).

If a name appears in several spellings (e.g., Kex and Ques) the principal entry should follow the most frequent spelling, with the other spellings listed to provide cross references to the main entry.

4. References

Each proper name should be followed by a reference to the line or paragraph where it first appears. For names which recur often, references to the first two or three mentions, followed by *passim*, will usually suffice for a narrative work. The summary section of the introduction will allow the reader to trace the adventures of the protagonists in an epic or romance. For an edition of lyric poems, however, the line references should ordinarily be complete.

5. Typefaces

As with the glossary, different typefaces should distinguish between the Old French names and the Modern French or English identifications.

6. Identifications

When dealing with an Old French epic or romance, an editor should consult Ernest Langlois, *Table des noms propres de toute nature compris dans les chansons de geste imprimées* (Paris, 1904); Louis-Fernand Flutre, *Table des noms propres avec toutes leurs variantes dans les romans français du moyen âge* (Poitiers, 1962); G. D. West, *An Index of Proper Names in French Arthurian Verse Romances, 1150–1300* (Toronto, 1969); and West, *French Arthurian Prose Romances: An Index of Proper Names* (Toronto, 1977).

Frequently identifications of character names will be restricted to information supplied by the work itself. Unless he was referring to well-known historical or legendary figures, a medieval author did not hesitate to use any name which he found useful or which caught his fancy.

Toponyms may be equally fanciful and hard to identify with real geographical places. "Lusarche" in the *Roman de Thèbes* (ed. Raynaud de Lage) remains a "ville non identifiée," and the efforts of scholars like P. Boissonnade and H. Grégoire to identify the place names in the Oxford *Roland* have been largely unsuccessful.

7. French Localities

If place names in France are to be identified in terms of modern *départements*, a recent map of the country should be consulted. During the 1960s several *départements* were renamed to avoid the supposedly pejorative adjectives *basses* and *inférieure*, and the *départements* surrounding Paris were restructured and renamed.

VI. SUPPLEMENTARY MATERIAL AND AIDS TO THE READER

1. Addenda and Corrigenda

An inserted sheet of corrections should be considered a last resort; it can usually be avoided by careful proofreading. Many readers will not bother to consult addenda and corrigenda.

2. Appendixes

An appendix is usually the best place for information drawn from the text and presented in list form: lengthy tables of assonances or rhymes, enumerations of proverbs and maxims, concordances with related texts, etc.

Also, in a critical edition, material which would interrupt a normal sequence of variants or notes should be relegated to an appendix. This applies to a particularly long variant—an interpolation or a *remaniement* of an episode—or to a note in danger of becoming a disquisition.

3. Illustrations

A plate reproducing a page from the basic manuscript will help the reader visualize the medieval appearance of the text he is reading.

4. Indexes

Like a glossary or a table of proper names, an index presents unconnected material in alphabetical sequence for single-item reference. The nature of the text and edition determines the need for an index. An edition which contains a long series of notes should list key words and topics in an index. For historical works, the text itself should be indexed.

5. Running Heads

Narrative texts, in verse or prose, are easier to follow or consult when running heads highlight the incidents recounted on the two facing pages below (see Faral's edition of Villehardouin). Sometimes it may prove convenient to have the running head on one page summarize the narrative while the other supplies line or paragraph numbers, possibly supplemented with line references to an earlier well-known edition; see, for example, the running heads of the Roques and Micha editions of Chrétien's romances, which provide summaries, line numbers, and references to the line numbers of the Foerster editions.

6. Table of Contents

French publishers customarily place the table of contents at the very end of the book, whereas in the U.S. and Great Britain it comes first, sometimes even before the preface. American editors who use French in their introduction, variants, and notes may choose either system; in many cases the editorial policy of a series determines the position of the table of contents.

The table of contents should list all the major divisions of the edition, including the titled subdivisions of the introduction (e.g., Author, Date of the Text, Title), as well as any material following the text (Variants, Notes, etc.).

Editors and Critical Editions

Armstrong, Edward C., et al., eds. *The Medieval French Roman d'Alexandre.* 7 vols. EM, 36–42. Princeton, 1937–76; rpt. (vols. 1–5, 7) 1965.

Bédier, Joseph, ed. *La Chanson de Roland.* 2 vols. Paris, 1922–27.

———. *Le Lai de l'Ombre par Jean Renart.* Fribourg, 1890; rpt. 1968.

———. *Le Lai de l'Ombre par Jean Renart.* SATF. Paris, 1913; rpt. 1966.

———. *Les Deux Poèmes de la Folie Tristan.* SATF. Paris, 1907; rpt. 1965.

Buffum, Douglas L., ed. Gerbert de Montreuil, *Le Roman de la Violette.* SATF. Paris, 1927.

Buridant, Claude, ed. *La Traduction du Pseudo-Turpin du manuscrit Vatican Regina 624.* PRF. Geneva, 1976.

Constans, Léopold, ed. *Le Roman de Thèbes.* 2 vols. SATF. Paris, 1890; rpt. 1968.

Corbett, Noel L., ed. Jehan de Joinville, *La Vie de saint Louis.* Sherbrooke, Québec, 1977.

Crist, Larry S., ed. *Saladin: Suite et fin du deuxième Cycle de la Croisade.* TLF. Geneva, 1972.

Delbouille, Maurice, ed. Henri d'Andeli, *Le Lai d'Aristote.* Bibliothèque de la Faculté de Philosophie et Lettres de l'Université de Liège. Paris, 1951.

Dembowski, Peter F., ed. *Jourdain de Blaye.* Chicago, 1969.

Ewert, Alfred, ed. Marie de France, *Lais.* Blackwell's French Texts. Oxford, 1944.

————. *Le Roman de Tristran* by Beroul. 2 vols. Oxford, 1939–70.

Faral, Edmond, ed. Villehardouin, *La Conquête de Constantinople*. 2 vols. Classiques de l'histoire de France au moyen âge. Paris, 1938–39.

————, and Julia Bastin, eds. Rutebeuf, *Œuvres Complètes*. 2 vols. Paris, 1959–60.

Foerster, Wendelin, ed. Kristian von Troyes, *Cligés, Yvain, Erec et Enide, Lancelot*. Halle, 1884, 1887, 1890, 1899.

Foulet, Alfred, ed. *Le Couronnement de Renard*. EM, 24. Princeton, 1929; rpt. 1965.

Frappier, Jean, trans. Chrétien de Troyes, *Le Chevalier de la Charrette*. 2nd ed. Paris, 1970.

Fukumoto, Naoyuki, ed. *Le Roman de Renart, Branches I et Ia*. Tokyo, 1974.

Guessard, Francis, ed. *Macaire*. APF. Paris, 1866; rpt. 1966.

————, and A. de Montaiglon, eds. *Aliscans*. APF. Paris, 1870; rpt. 1966.

————, and Paul Meyer, eds. *Aye d'Avignon*. APF. Paris, 1861; rpt. 1966.

————, and Léon Gautier, eds. *La Chanson d'Aspremont*. Paris, 1855.

————, and Polycarpe Chabaille, eds. *Gaufrey*. APF. Paris, 1859; rpt. 1966.

————, and Siméon Luce, eds. *Gaydon*. APF. Paris, 1862; rpt. 1966.

————, and H. Michelant, eds. *Gui de Bourgogne, Otinel, Floovant*. APF. Paris, 1858; rpt. 1966.

————, and C. Grandmaison, eds. *Huon de Bordeaux*. APF. Paris, 1860; rpt. 1966.

————, and Lorédan Larchey, eds. *Parise la Duchesse*. APF. Paris, 1860; rpt. 1966.

Ham, Edward B., ed. *Jehan le Venelais (Nevelon), La Venjance Alixandre*. Ann Arbor, 1946.

Henry, Albert, ed. Adenet le Roi, *Œuvres*. 5 tomes in 6 vols. Bruges, Paris, Brussels, 1951–71.

————. *Chrestomathie de la littérature en ancien français*. 5th ed. Berne, 1970.

————. Jehan Bodel, *Le Jeu de saint Nicolas*. Travaux de la Faculté de Philosophie et Lettres de l'Université libre de Bruxelles. 2nd ed. Brussels, 1965.

Holmes, Urban T., Jr., ed. Adenet le Roi, *Berte aus grans pies*. UNCSRLL. Chapel Hill, 1946.

Kroeber, A., and G. Servois, eds. *Fierabras*. APF. Paris, 1860; rpt. 1966.

McMillan, Duncan, ed. *Le Charroi de Nîmes*. BFR. Paris, 1972.

Méon, D. M., ed. *Fabliaux et contes des poètes françois*. 4 vols. Paris, 1808.

——. *Le Roman de Renart*. 4 vols. Paris, 1826. *Supplément*, ed. Polycarpe Chabaille. Paris, 1835.

Meyer, Paul, ed. *Girart de Roussillon* (never completed).

——. *Gui de Nanteuil*. APF. Paris, 1861; rpt. 1966.

Micha, Alexandre, ed. *Chrétien de Troyes, Cligés*. CFMA. Paris, 1965.

Michel, Francisque, ed. *La Chanson de Roland*. Paris, 1837.

——. *Lais inédits des XIIe et XIIIe siècles*. Paris, 1836.

——. *Mémoires de Jean de Joinville*. Paris, 1830, 1858.

Mills, Leonard R., ed. *Barlaam et Josaphat*. TLF. Geneva, 1973.

Misrahi, Jean, ed. *Le Roman des Sept Sages*. Paris, 1933; rpt. 1975.

Noomen, Willem, ed. *Le Jeu d'Adam*. CFMA. Paris, 1971.

Palermo, Joseph, ed. *Le Roman de Cassidorus*. 2 vols. SATF. Paris, 1963–64.

Paris, Gaston, ed. *La Vie de saint Alexis*. CFMA. 7th ed. Paris, 1911; rpt. 1965.

——. *La Vie de saint Léger. Romania*, 1 (1872), 273–317.

——, and Léopold Pannier, eds. *La Vie de saint Alexis*. BÉHÉ. Paris, 1872.

Plomp, H. P. B., ed. *Le Roman des Sept Sages en prose* (Paris, B.N. fr. 95). *De Middelnederlandsche bewerking van het gedicht van den binnen Rome*, Appendix. Utrecht, 1899.

Raynaud, Gaston, ed. *La Chastelaine de Vergi*. CFMA. Paris, 1910.

Raynaud de Lage, Guy, ed. *Le Roman de Thèbes*. 2 vols. CFMA. Paris, 1966–68.

Régnier, Claude, ed. *La Prise d'Orange*. BFR. 3rd ed. Paris, 1970.

Roach, William, ed. *Chrétien de Troyes, Le Roman de Perceval ou le Conte du Graal*. TLF. 2nd ed. Geneva, 1959.

——, et al., eds. *The Continuations of the Old French 'Perceval' of Chrétien de Troyes*. 4 vols. Philadelphia, 1949–71.

Roques, Mario, ed. *Aucassin et Nicolette*. CFMA. Paris, 1929.

——. *Chrétien de Troyes, Erec et Enide*. CFMA. Paris, 1963.

——. *Chrétien de Troyes, Le Chevalier au lion (Yvain)*. CFMA. Paris, 1960.

——. *Chrétien de Troyes, Le Chevalier de la Charrete*. CFMA. Paris, 1958.

——. *Le Roman de Renart*. 6 vols. CFMA. Paris, 1951–63.

Rychner, Jean. *Contribution à l'étude des fabliaux*. 2 vols. Neuchâtel, 1960.

——, ed. *Eustache d'Amiens, Du Bouchier d'Abevile*. TLF. Geneva, 1975.

———. Marie de France, *Lais*. CFMA. Paris, 1973.

———. Marie de France, *Lanval*. TLF. Geneva, 1958.

Segre, Cesare, ed. *La Chanson de Roland*. Milan, 1971.

Stengel, Edmund, ed. *Das altfranzösische Rolandslied*, I (vol. II never published). Leipzig, 1900.

Viard, Jules, ed. *Les Grandes Chroniques de France*. 10 vols. Société de l'Histoire de France. Paris, 1920–53.

Wailly, Natalis de, ed. Joinville, *Histoire de saint Louis*. Paris, 1868; rev. ed., 1874.

Warnke, Karl, ed. Marie de France, *Lais*. Halle, 1885.

Whitehead, Frederick, ed. *La Chastelaine de Vergi*. 2nd ed. Manchester, Eng., 1951.

Selective Reference Bibliography

N.B.: Items marked with an asterisk deal specifically with Old French texts.

A. THEORY AND METHODS OF TEXTUAL CRITICISM

1. Andrieu, Jean. "Principes et recherches en critique textuelle." In *Mémorial des études latines* . . . *offert* . . . *à* . . . *J. Marouzeau*, pp. 458–74. Paris, 1943.
2. Avalle, D'Arco Silvio. *Principî di critica testuale.* Vulgares eloquentes, 7. Padua, 1972.
3. Barbi, Michele. *La nuova filologia e l'edizione dei nostri scrittori da Dante al Manzoni.* Florence, 1938; rpt. 1973.
*4. Bédier, Joseph. "De l'édition princeps de la *Chanson de Roland* aux éditions les plus récentes: nouvelles remarques sur l'art d'établir les anciens textes." *Romania,* 63 (1937), 433–69; 64 (1938), 145–244, 489–521. Cf. Mario Roques's index of *Roland* references in *Romania,* 66 (1940–41), 371–75.
*5. ————. "La Tradition manuscrite du *Lai de l'Ombre*: réflexions sur l'art d'éditer les anciens textes." *Romania,* 54 (1928), 161–96, 321–56. Rpt. as pamphlet, Paris, 1970.
*6. ————, ed. *Le Lai de l'Ombre.* Fribourg, 1890. Reviewed by Gaston Paris, *Romania,* 19 (1890), 609–15.
*7. ————, ed. *Le Lai de l'Ombre par Jean Renart.* SATF. Paris, 1913.

8. Bieler, Ludwig. *The Grammarian's Craft: An Introduction to Textual Criticism.* New York, 1965 (rpt. from *Classical Folia*, 10 [1958], 3–42).

9. Bowers, Fredson. "Textual Criticism." *Encyclopaedia Britannica*, XXI, 918–23. Chicago, 1967.

10. ———. "Textual Criticism." In *The Aims and Methods of Scholarship in Modern Languages and Literatures*, edited by James Thorpe, pp. 23–42. New York, 1963.

11. Brambilla Ageno, Franca. *L'edizione critica dei testi volgari.* Medioevo e umanésimo, 22. Padua, 1975. Review by Mary B. Speer, to appear in *RPh*, 32 (Feb. 1979).

*12. Castellani, Arrigo. *Bédier avait-il raison? La Méthode de Lachmann dans les éditions de textes du moyen âge.* Discours Universitaires, n.s. 20. Fribourg, 1957. Reviewed by E. B. Ham, *RPh*, 13 (1959–60), 190–91.

13. Chiari, Alberto. "L'edizione critica." In *Tecnica e teoria letteraria*, edited by M. Fubini, G. Getto, B. Migliorini, A. Chiari, and V. Pernicone, pp. 231–95. 2nd ed. Milan, 1951.

14. Clark, Albert C. *Recent Developments in Textual Criticism.* Oxford, 1914.

15. ———. *The Descent of Manuscripts.* Oxford, 1918.

*16. Coculesco, P. S. "Sur les méthodes de critique textuelle du type Lachmann-Quentin." *Grai şi Suflet*, 4 (1929–30), 97–107.

17. Collomp, Paul. *La Critique des textes.* Publications de la Faculté des Lettres de Strasbourg, Initiation et Méthode, fasc. 6. Paris, 1931.

18. Dain, Alphonse. "L'Edition des textes et le problème de l'utilisation des manuscrits." *Information Littéraire*, 3 (1951), 99–104.

19. ———. *Les Manuscrits.* Collection d'études anciennes. 2nd ed. Paris, 1964.

20. Dearing, V. A. *Methods of Textual Editing.* Los Angeles, 1962.

21. De Robertis, Domenico. "Problemi di metodo nell'edizione dei cantari." In no. 52, pp. 119–38.

*22. Ecole des chartes. *Livre du centenaire (1821–1921).* 2 vols. Paris, 1921.

*23. Ewert, Alfred. "On Textual Criticism, with Special Reference to Anglo-Norman." *Arthuriana*, 2 (1929–30), 56–69.

*24. Fourquet, Jean. "Fautes communes ou innovations communes?" *Romania*, 70 (1948–49), 85–95.

*25. ———. "Le Paradoxe de Bédier." *Mélanges 1945.* II, *Etudes littéraires*, pp. 1–16. Publications de la Faculté de Lettres de l'Université de Strasbourg, fasc. 105. Paris, 1946. Reviewed by Roques, Romania, 69 (1946–47), 116–17.

26. Froger, Dom J. La Critique des textes et son automatisation. Initiation aux nouveautés de la science, 7. Paris, 1968.

27. Grafton, Anthony C. "Joseph Scaliger's Edition of Catullus (1577) and the Traditions of Textual Criticism in the Renaissance." Journal of the Warburg and Courtauld Institutes, 38 (1975), 155–81.

*28. Grigsby, John L. "A Defense and Four Illustrations of Textual Criticism." RPh, 20 (1966–67), 500–520.

*29. Ham, Edward B. "Textual Criticism and Common Sense." RPh, 12 (1958–59), 198–215.

*30. ———. Textual Criticism and Jehan le Venelais. Ann Arbor, 1946.

*31. Heinemann, Edward A. "Sur la valeur des manuscrits rimés pour l'étude de la tradition rolandienne: tentative pour trouver les filiations des manuscrits TLP." Le Moyen Age, 80 (1974), 71–87.

32. Housman, A. E. Selected Prose. Edited by John Carter. Cambridge, 1961.

33. Irigoin, Jean. "Stemmas bifides et états de manuscrits." Revue de Philologie, 3ᵉ série, 28 (1954), 211–17.

34. Kane, George. "Conjectural Emendation." In Medieval Literature and Civilization: Studies in Memory of G. N. Garmonsway, pp. 155–69. London, 1969. Rpt. in no. 36, pp. 211–25.

35. Kenney, E. J. "Textual Criticism." Encyclopaedia Britannica, Macropaedia, XVIII, 189–95. Chicago, 1975.

*36. Kleinhenz, Christopher, ed. Medieval Manuscripts and Textual Criticism. UNCSRLL; Symposia, 4. Chapel Hill, 1976.

*37. Legge, M. Dominica. "Recent Methods of Textual Criticism." Arthuriana, 2 (1929–30), 48–55.

38. Maas, Paul. Textkritik. Einleitung in die Altertumswissenschaft, I. 3rd ed. Leipzig, 1957. English translation by Barbara Flower; Oxford, 1958.

*39. Marichal, Robert. "La Critique des textes." In L'Histoire et ses méthodes, edited by Charles Samaran, pp. 1247–1366. Encyclopédie de la Pléiade, XI. Paris, 1961.

*40. Micha, Alexandre. Prolégomènes à une édition de 'Cligès.' Annales de l'Université de Lyon, 3ᵉ série, fasc. 8. Paris, 1938.

*41. ———. La Tradition manuscrite des romans de Chrétien de Troyes. Paris, 1939; rpt. 1966.

*42. Paris, Gaston, and Léopold Pannier, eds. La Vie de saint Alexis, *poème du XIᵉ siècle et renouvellements des XIIᵉ, XIIIᵉ et XIVᵉ siècles.* BÉHÉ. Paris, 1872.

43. Pasquali, Giorgio. *Storia della tradizione critica del testo.* Florence, 1934; rpt. 1952. Reviewed by Dain, *Supplément critique au Bulletin de l'Association Guillaume Budé,* 8 (1936–37), 7–32.

44. Peckham, Lawton P. G. "Editing and Textual Criticism." In "The Aims, Methods, and Materials of Research in the Modern Languages and Literatures." *PMLA,* 67 (1952), 15–19.

45. Peeters, Félix. "Les Différents Systèmes de classement des manuscrits." *Revue de l'Université de Bruxelles,* 1930–31, 466–85.

*46. Quentin, Dom Henri. *Essais de critique textuelle (Ecdotique).* Paris, 1926.

*47. Reid, T. B. W. "Chrétien de Troyes and the Scribe Guiot." *Medium Ævum,* 45 (1976), 1–19.

*48. ———. "On the Text of the *Tristran* of Béroul." In *Medieval Miscellany Presented to Eugène Vinaver,* pp. 263–88. Manchester, Eng., 1965. Rpt. in no. 36, pp. 245–71.

49. Reynolds, Leighton D., and Nigel G. Wilson. *Scribes and Scholars: A Guide to the Transmission of Greek and Latin Literature.* 2nd ed. Oxford, 1974.

*50. Roncaglia, Aurelio. "Critica testuale." *Cultura neolatina,* 12 (1952), 281–83.

*51. Shepard, William P. "Recent Theories of Textual Criticism." *Modern Philology,* 28 (1930), 129–41.

52. Spongano, Raffaele, ed. *Studi e problemi di critica testuale.* Convegno di Studi di Filologia italiana nel Centenario della Commissione per i Testi di Lingua, 7–9 aprile 1960. Bologna, 1961.

*53. Timpanaro, Sebastiano. *La genesi del metodo del Lachmann.* Bibliotechina del saggiatore, 18. Florence, 1963.

*54. Vàrvaro, Alberto. "Critica dei testi classica e romanza. Problemi comuni ed esperienze diverse." *Rendiconti della Accademia de Archeologia, Lettere e Belle Arti di Napoli,* 45 (1970), 73–117.

*55. Vinaver, Eugène. "Principles of Textual Emendation." In *Studies in French Language and Mediaeval Literature Presented to Mildred K. Pope,* pp. 351–69. Manchester, Eng., 1939. Rpt. in no. 36, pp. 139–59.

*56. Walberg, Emmanuel. "Prinzipien und Methoden für die Herausgabe alter Texte nach verschiedenen Handschriften." *Zeitschrift für Romanische Philologie,* 51 (1931), 665–78.

57. West, Martin L. *Textual Criticism and Editorial Technique Applicable to Greek and Latin Texts*. Stuttgart, 1973.
*58. Whitehead, Frederick. "The Textual Criticism of the *Chanson de Roland*: An Historical Review." In *Studies in Medieval French Presented to Alfred Ewert*, pp. 76–89. Oxford, 1961.
*59. ———, and Cedric E. Pickford. "The Introduction to the *Lai de l'Ombre*: Sixty Years Later." *Romania*, 94 (1973), 145–56. Rpt. in no. 36, pp. 103–15.
*60. ———. "The Two-Branch Stemma." *BBSIA*, 3 (1951), 83–90.
61. Willis, James. *Latin Textual Criticism*. Urbana, Ill., 1972.
*62. Wilmotte, Maurice. "Sur la critique des textes." In *Etudes de philologie wallonne*, pp. 3–38. Paris, 1932.
*63. Zumthor, Paul. *Essai de poétique médiévale*. Paris, 1972.

B. GUIDELINES FOR CRITICAL AND DIPLOMATIC EDITIONS

See nos. *2, 11, 13, 17, 29, 35, 38, 39*.
*64. Brunel, Clovis. "A propos de l'édition de nos textes français du moyen âge." *Bulletin de la Société de l'Histoire de France*, 1941–42, 67–74.
65. Contini, Gianfranco. "Rapporti fra la filologia (come critica testuale) e la linguistica romanza." *Actes du XIIème Congrès International de Linguistique et Philologie romanes*. I, 47–65. Bucharest, 1970.
66. Dekkers, Dom Eligius. "La Tradition des textes et les problèmes de l'édition diplomatique." *Traditio*, 10 (1954), 549–55.
67. Grat, Félix. "L'Histoire des textes et des éditions critiques." *BEC*, 94 (1933), 296–309.
68. Havet, Louis. *Règles et recommandations générales pour l'établissement des éditions Guillaume Budé*. Chartres, n.d.
*69. Knudson, Charles A. "The Publication of Old French Texts: Some Comments and Suggestions." *Speculum*, 24 (1949), 510–15.
70. Masai, François. "Principes et conventions de l'édition diplomatique." *Scriptorium*, 4 (1950), 177–93.
*71. Meyer, Paul. "Instruction pour la publication des anciens textes." *Bulletin de la Société des Anciens Textes Français*, 34 (1908), 64–79. Rpt. in *BEC*, 71 (1910), 224–33.
72. Moorman, Charles. *Editing the Middle English Manuscript*. Jackson, Miss., 1975.

*73. Roques, Mario. "Etablissement de règles pratiques pour l'édition des anciens textes français et provençaux." Paris, 1926. Rpt. in *Romania*, 52 (1926), 243–49, and in *BEC*, 87 (1926), 453–59.

74. Rossini, Egidio. "Introduction to the Edition of Medieval Vernacular Documents (XIII and XIV Centuries)." In no. 36, pp. 175–210.

75. "The Center for Scholarly Editions: An Introductory Statement." *PMLA*, 92 (1977), 583–97.

C. HANDLING THE MANUSCRIPTS

See nos. 15, 17, 18, 19, 48, 55, 61.

76. Andrieu, Jean. "Pour l'explication psychologique des fautes de copiste." *Revue des Etudes Latines*, 28 (1950), 279–92.

*77. Blakey, Brian. "The Scribal Process." In *Medieval Miscellany Presented to Eugène Vinaver*, pp. 19–27. Manchester, Eng., 1965.

*78. Carroll, Carleton W. "Medieval Romance Paleography: An Introduction." In no. 36, pp. 39–82.

79. Castellani, Arrigo. "Indagine sugli errori di trascrizione." In no. 52, pp. 35–40. Rpt., translated by Anthony Bouchard, in no. 36, pp. 167–73.

*80. Chaytor, H. J. *From Script to Print*. Cambridge, 1945; rpt. 1966.

81. Diringer, David. *The Hand-Produced Book*. London, 1953.

82. Havet, Louis. *Manuel de critique verbale appliquée aux textes latins*. Paris, 1911.

*83. Kennedy, Elspeth. "The Scribe as Editor." In *Mélanges de langue et de littérature du moyen âge et de la renaissance offerts à Jean Frappier*, I, 523–31. Geneva, 1970.

*84. Omont, Henri, and Philippe Lauer. *Liste des recueils de facsimilés et des reproductions de manuscrits conservés à la Bibliothèque nationale*. 3rd ed. Paris, 1935.

85. Pollard, Graham. "Describing Medieval Bookbinding." In *Medieval Learning and Literature: Essays Presented to Richard William Hunt*, pp. 50–65. Oxford, 1976.

*86. Prou, Maurice. *Manuel de paléographie latine et française*. 4th ed. Paris, 1924.

*87. Raynaud de Lage, Guy. "Retouches au lexique du *Roman de Thèbes*." In *Mélanges de philologie et de linguistique offerts* à *Tauno Nurmela*, pp. 161–67. Turku, 1967. Rpt. in *Les Premiers Romans français*, pp. 191–97. Geneva, 1976.

*88. Roques, Mario. "Le Manuscrit 794 de la Bibliothèque Nationale et le scribe Guiot." *Romania*, 73 (1952), 177–99.

*89. Rychner, Jean. *Contribution à l'étude des fabliaux: Variantes, remaniements, dégradations*. I, *Observations*; II, *Textes*. Neuchâtel, 1960.

*90. Samaran, Charles. "La Recherche des manuscrits d'auteurs du moyen âge et de la renaissance." *Revue du Seizième Siècle*, 15 (1928), 344–55.

*91. Segre, Cesare. "La première 'scène du cor' dans la *Chanson de Roland* et la méthode de travail des copistes." In *Mélanges offerts à Rita Lejeune*, II, 871–89. Gembloux, 1969.

*92. Stiennon, Jacques, and Geneviève Hasenohr. *Paléographie du moyen âge*. Collection U, Série Histoire médiévale. Paris, 1973.

*93. Stones, M. Alison. "Secular Manuscript Illumination in France." In no. 36, pp. 83–102.

D. SPECIAL PROBLEMS IN PREPARING THE TEXT OF A CRITICAL EDITION

See nos. 11, 34, 43, 47, 52, 55.

*94. Acher, Jean. "De l'emploi du tréma." *Revue des Langues Romanes*, 56 (1913), 458–65.

*95. ———. "Sur l'*x* finale des manuscrits." *Revue des Langues Romanes*, 56 (1913), 148–58.

*96. Edwards, Bateman. *A Classification of the Manuscripts of Gui de Cambrai's 'Vengement Alixandre,'* esp. pp. 12–24. EM, 20. Princeton, 1926.

*97. Faral, Edmond. "A propos de l'édition des textes anciens: le cas du manuscrit unique." In *Recueil de travaux offert à M. Clovis Brunel*, I, 409–21. Paris, 1955.

*98. Frank, István. "De l'art d'éditer les textes lyriques." In *Recueil de travaux offert à M. Clovis Brunel*, I, 463–75. Paris, 1955. Rpt., translated by Arnold Miller, in no. 36, pp. 123–38.

99. Roncaglia, Aurelio. "Valore e giuoco dell'interpretazione nella critica testuale." In no. 52, pp. 45–62. Rpt., translated by Giancarlo Maiorino, in no. 36, pp. 227–44.

*100. Rothwell, W. "Appearance and reality in Anglo-Norman." In

Studies in Medieval Literature and Languages in Memory of Frederick Whitehead, pp. 239–56. Manchester, Eng., 1973.

*101. Segre, Cesare. "Appunti sul problema delle contaminazioni nei testi in prosa." In no. 52, pp. 63–67. Rpt., translated by Kleinhenz, in no. 36, pp. 117–22.

E. DICTIONARIES AND GRAMMARS

*102. Foerster, Wendelin, and Hermann Breuer. Wörterbuch zu Kristian von Troyes' sämtlichen Werken. Halle, 1964.

*103. Fouché, Pierre. Le Verbe français; étude morphologique. Tradition de l'Humanisme, IV. 2nd ed. Paris, 1967.

*104. ———. Phonétique historique du français. 3 vols. 2nd ed. Paris, 1966–69.

*105. Foulet, Lucien. Glossary of the First Continuation of the Old French 'Perceval' of Chrétien de Troyes, edited by William Roach. Vol. III, part 2. Philadelphia, 1955.

*106. ———. Petite Syntaxe de l'ancien français. CFMA. 3rd ed. Paris, 1930.

*107. Gossen, Charles Théodore. Grammaire de l'ancien picard. BFR. Paris, 1970.

*108. Godefroy, Frédéric. Dictionnaire de l'ancien français et de tous ses dialectes du IXe au XVe siècle. 10 vols. Paris, 1881–1902; rpt. 1962.

*109. ———. Lexique de l'ancien français. Paris, 1901; rpt. 1967.

*110. Greimas, A. J. Dictionnaire de l'ancien français jusqu'au milieu du XIVe siècle. Paris, 1967.

*111. La Curne de Sainte-Palaye. Dictionnaire historique de l'ancien langage français. 10 vols. Paris, 1875–82.

*112. Ménard, Philippe. Syntaxe. Vol. III of Manuel de l'ancien français, edited by Yves Lefèvre. Paris, 1968.

*113. Moignet, Gérard. Grammaire de l'ancien français; morphologie, syntaxe. Initiation à la linguistique; Série B, Problèmes et Méthodes, 2. Paris, 1973.

*114. Pope, Mildred K. From Latin to Modern French. 2nd ed. Manchester, Eng., 1952; rpt. 1966.

*115. Raynaud de Lage, Guy. Introduction à l'ancien français. SEDES. 7th ed. Paris, 1973.

*116. Schwan, Eduard, and Dietrich Behrens. Grammaire de l'ancien français, translated by Oscar Bloch. 4th ed., based on 11th German ed. Leipzig, 1932.

*117. Tobler, Adolf. *Vom französischen Versbau alter und neuer Zeit.*
       5th ed. Leipzig, 1910.
*118. ———, and Erhard Lommatzsch. *Altfranzösisches Wörterbuch.*
       Berlin, 1925–.
*119. Verrier, Paul Isidore. *Le Vers français.* 3 vols. Bibliothèque de
       la Société des amis de l'Université de Paris. Paris, 1931–32.
*120. Wacker, Gertrud. *Über das Verhältnis von Dialekt und Schrift-
       sprache im Altfranzösischen.* Beiträge zur Geschichte der ro-
       manischen Sprachen und Literaturen, XI. Halle, 1916.

Index

129

versy concerning, 23–35; defense of, by classicists and new philologists, 23–27, 32–34; description of, 8–10, 49–50, 52–56; development of, 8; limitations of, 16–20, 22, 57; refinement of, by Dom Quentin, 20–22, 25–26

Lacunas: signaling, in critical apparatus, 96; as significant errors, 54, 56; supplying the text for, from another manuscript, 76, 85

Lai d'Aristote (Henri d'Andeli), 35, 85, 108–9

Lai de l'Ombre (Jean Renart): Bédier's composite edition of (1890), 18–19; Bédier's conservative edition of (1913), 2 n. 3, 8 n. 8, 18 n. 22, 19–20, 24, 31, 34–35; Michel's edition of, 4; Dom Quentin's stemma for, 21–22; unnamed characters in, for table of proper names, 109

Lais (Marie de France), 36, 64, 67, 77, 85, 89

Lambert le Tort, 90

Lancelot (Chrétien de Troyes), 24, 28 n. 29, 43, 58, 109

Langlois, Ernest, 110

Language: of author, 87, 92–93, 104; of scribe, 87, 93

Lanval (Marie de France), 36, 67, 85

Le Clerc, Jean, 83

Lectio difficilior, 82–84, 103

Legge, M. Dominica, 23, 25

Localities, French, 111

Locus desperatus, 84, 103

Luce, Siméon, 5 n. 5, 7

Maas, Paul, 26, 32

Macaire, 5 n. 5, 7

McMillan, Duncan, 94, 97

Manuscript, basic: choosing, 20, 22, 24, 33–34, 35–39, 47–50, 55–56, 87, 94–95, 101–2; describing, 87, 94; grooming, 76–85; illustrating, with plate, 112; readings rejected from, 95–96; use of controllers

with, 36–37, 50, 95. *See also* Archetype; Lachmann method; Stemma codicum

Manuscript, best: adherence to, in empirical period, 4–9; Bédier's doctrine of conserving, 20, 22, 24, 27–29, 32–34, 38; choosing, 49–50, 57; editions based on, 20, 38

Manuscript, original, 9–10, 11, 28–29, 31, 32–33, 35, 41, 47, 49–50

Marichal, Robert, 25–26, 34

Marie de France, 36, 77, 85, 89

Ménard, Philippe, 66–67, 93

Méon, D. M., 3–4

Meyer, Paul: as advocate of Lachmann method, 10–11, 12 n. 13; as empirical editor, 5 n. 5; his reservations about Lachmann method, 15–18; his rules for editors, xiii

Micha, Alexandre, 36–37, 80, 112

Michelant, H., 5 n. 5, 6–7

Michel, Francisque, 4–5, 10 n. 11, 12 n. 13

Microfilms, 45–46, 47, 49

Middle French, characteristics of, 93

Mills, Leonard, 77

Misrahi, Jean, 62

Moignet, Gérard, 93

Morel, Charles, 10

Mortier, Raoul, 44

Müller, Theodore, 37

Nasalization, bar of, 78

New philology, Italian school of, 25 n. 25, 32–34

Nibelungenlied, 10

Nicol, Henry, 16–17

Noomen, Willem, 64

Normalization, problems of, 76–85

Notes to an edition, 76, 78, 84, 90, 92, 103–4

Numbering sections of a text, 74–76

Numerals, Roman, in text, 62, 63

Omont, Henri, 43

Otinel, 5 n. 5, 6